DAILY TASTE

of

Proverbs

Wisdom
for the Busy
Person

John W. Stanko

A Daily Taste of Proverbs
by John W. Stanko
Copyright © 2014 John W. Stanko

ISBN 978-1-63360-001-0
For Worldwide Distribution
Printed in the U.S.A.

PurposeQuest Ink
P.O. Box 8881 · Pittsburgh, PA 15221-0881
412.646.2780

12/25/14

Taste + see that the
Lord is good!

Jill M Stal

Prov 2:2-5

Ps 37:8

INTRODUCTION

In 1997, I wrote a book entitled *A Daily Dose of Proverbs: Wisdom for Contemporary Living.* It is my best-seller to date (also available in Kindle version), although not in huge numbers. Perhaps that is because in 2009, I started an online version of the daily devotional. I first started to publish the abbreviated version when I joined the staff at Allegheny Center Alliance Church as the pastor for discipleship. The staff there did not know me very well, so I thought I would send them a daily devotional to help them understand me and my love for the book of Proverbs. Then I started posting those daily devotionals on my personal website, and that was the foundation for what you are either holding in your hand or reading from your e-reader.

While my first book was a verse from Proverbs for every day of the year along with a page of devotional material, this *A Daily Taste of Proverbs* has a completely different format. I used the same verse for the day that I had used in the original book – that remained the same. After that it's all new. The devotional material in *A Daily Taste* is much shorter. I inserted questions to help you, the reader, understand and apply what I wrote. Finally, I included a cross reference from another part of the Bible to help you better grasp the meaning and application of the verse for that day.

I am especially pleased that I was able to link these 366 'tastes' to every other book in the Bible at least once. You can see that for yourself in the Appendix that contains a list of the cross references by day and verse. I think this is important for two reasons. One, all Scripture is interrelated and that's important to keep in mind as we read and study God's Word. Second, the book of Proverbs can seem to have such unique material that it stands all by itself as biblical wisdom literature. I hope I show that is not the case where Proverbs is concerned. I have to admit the challenge of linking all 65 books to Proverbs was fun and a good way for me to study Scripture; I hope you find it the same.

I continue to study Proverbs as part of my life's work, and I know that modern people need the timeless wisdom in Proverbs as much as ever – as I do. I also realize that 21st century readers are much less inclined to spend long amounts of time in study, especially on a daily basis. That is why I shortened these devotionals to provide busy people the chance to spend a few minutes reading and then looking at another part of the Bible from just one verse of Proverbs. I would think families could use this at breakfast, in the car on the way to school, at dinnertime or for personal study.

However you choose to use this book, I suggest that you have two other tools by your side as you go. One would be your Bible to look up the cross references and the other is a journal to record your thoughts and responses to the questions I pose.

So there you have my reasoning for *A Daily Taste of Proverbs* as a sequel to *A Daily Dose of Proverbs*. I hope that both books become a part of your regular devotional repertoire, and that you will devote additional time to study God's wisdom literature, of which Proverbs is the crown jewel. Thank you, and may the Lord bless the reading and study of His word!

John Stanko
Pittsburgh, PA
April, 2014

A Daily Taste Of Proverbs

January

January 1
Proverbs 1:3

"For acquiring a disciplined and prudent life, doing what is right and just and fair."

A good and productive life doesn't just happen. It takes planning, hard work and God's grace. **What are your goals this year to improve your quality of life and be more disciplined?** Set goals in as many areas as possible - financial, health, spiritual, personal development and family. Let Joshua 24:13-14 be your theme as you grow and improve your faithfulness.

January 2
Proverbs 2:6

"For the Lord gives wisdom, and from his mouth come knowledge and understanding."

Wisdom is a gift from God. You cannot earn it but you can position yourself to receive it. What's more, God is always communicating His wisdom. **Are you listening for Him? Do you expect answers to your problems and questions?** Solomon asked for wisdom in 1 Kings 3:5-15 and God gave it. **Why don't you ask, too?**

January 3
Proverbs 3:19

"By wisdom the Lord laid the earth's foundations, by understanding he set the heavens in place."

Wisdom enables you to do creative things in fresh ways. Therefore wisdom is not what you know but rather what you do with what you know. **What are you doing with**

your wisdom? What evidence is there that you have some? Where in life do you need more? 1 Samuel 25 shows wisdom in action by a woman named Abigail.

January 4
Proverbs 4:3-4

"When I was a boy in my father's house, still tender, and an only child of my mother, He taught me."

It is never too early to teach a child about the Lord and His ways. **What are you doing to prepare the next generation to serve the Lord? What about your own children, nieces and nephews? What more can you do to instruct them or children in your church?** Read what Jesus said about little children in Matthew 19:14.

January 5
Proverbs 5:23

"He will die for lack of discipline,
led astray by his own great folly."

You pay a price if you lack discipline. Usually the loss is not from what you do but rather what you don't do. **What has lack of discipline cost you in lost opportunities? What can you start today that by next year you will have done something you always wanted to do?** 2 Samuel 11 shows the discipline of Bathsheba's husband Uriah and the lack on the part of King David.

January 6
Proverbs 6:20

"My son, keep your father's commands
and do not forsake your mother's teaching."

Parents need to teach and children need taught. **What were your parents' favorite sayings or warnings? What are yours for your children? Are you living in a consistent manner with what you were taught or are teaching?** Whether a parent or child, you can read Colossians 3:20-21 and Deuteronomy 11:19 to review your duties and responsibilities toward one another.

January 7
Proverbs 7:1

"My son, keep my words
and store up my commands within you."

No matter your circumstances, God expects you to keep His commands. If money is tight, you must still be generous. If others are cheating, you must maintain your integrity. If others are mean-spirited, you are to be kind. **What are you doing to store (and then obey) the commands of God in your life?** As a good example of this, consider what Daniel went through yet how he stayed true to the Lord in Daniel 1:3-8.

January 8
Proverbs 8:34

"Blessed is the man who listens to me, watching daily at my doors, waiting at my doorway."

Listening, watching and waiting are not passive postures. **What are you doing to access wisdom? What are you reading, studying, watching or doing? With whom do you spend time?** If you seek wisdom, you will be rewarded! Read Paul's charge in 2 Timothy 2:14-26 and notice the effort it takes to grow in wisdom and effectiveness. **Are you ready to pay the price?**

January 9
Proverbs 9:10

"The fear of the Lord is the beginning of wisdom, and knowledge of the Holy One is understanding."

Never make a decision based on what's best for you, but rather on what is God's best for you. That requires that you know God, which can only happen as you know and apply His word. David wrote and sang about the power of the Word in your life in Psalm 18:30-36. **Are you applying God's word effectively in your life, work, family and ministry?**

January 10
Proverbs 10:6

"Blessings crown the head of the righteous, but violence overwhelms the mouth of the wicked."

You can have confidence in God's ability to bless and protect you. Consider Rahab, who hid Joshua's spies and was spared when Israel attacked her city. What's more, Rahab ended up in Jesus' family tree. That is a great example of how God can protect and bless you! **Are you trusting in Him or giving in to unwarranted fears?** To read more about Rahab, see Joshua 2, Joshua 6:25 and Matthew 1:5.

January 11
Proverbs 11:2

"When pride comes, then comes disgrace, but with humility comes wisdom."

When you are dependent on God and others, you open

yourself to answers and help beyond your abilities and experience. When you stubbornly say, "I can handle this" when you can't, you set yourself up for failure and disgrace. **Are you disguising pride as something else, like not wanting to bother others with your problems?** To see the power of humility, read what Nineveh did in response to Jonah's preaching in Jonah 3. They humbled themselves and God spared their lives!

January 12
Proverbs 12:8

"A man is praised according to his wisdom, but men with warped minds are despised."

In order to have and disseminate wisdom, you must have correct thinking and that requires confronting your incorrect thinking. **What are you doing to bring about the change of thinking necessary for growth and wisdom in your life, work and relationships?** Jesus said in Matthew 22:36-38 that you are to love God with all your mind. **Do you, or is your thought life a mess?**

January 13
Proverbs 13:13

"He who scorns instruction will pay for it, but he who respects a command is rewarded."

Learning is a way of life, not an event. You never outgrow your need to be taught, learn and then teach. **Do you have a teachable spirit? Do you apply what you learn? Do you look for opportunities to teach others, which in and of itself helps you to grow and learn?** Read Hebrews 5:11-14 to see what God's teaching expectations are for you as a mature believer.

January 14
Proverbs 14:11

---

*"The house of the wicked will be destroyed,
but the tent of the upright will flourish."*

Your actions and decisions have implications not only for you, but also for those closest to you. **Are you creating an environment in your home, work or ministry that God can bless and where people can grow?** Joshua made a decision that his household would serve the Lord in Joshua 24:14-15 and the Philippian jailer did the same in Acts 16:29:34. Their commitment carried over to those around them and yours should too!

January 15
Proverbs 15:1

---

*"A gentle answer turns away wrath,
but a harsh word stirs up anger."*

Jesus said your heart speaks through your mouth. Thus you communicate not only with your words, but also through your tone, volume, inflection, facial expressions and body language. **If you receive angry or annoying responses more often than not, are you in any way the source of the problem?** You can read what Jesus said in Luke 6:45 and then what Paul wrote about the matter in Ephesians 4:29-32.

January 16
Proverbs 16:19

---

*"Better to be lowly in spirit and among the
oppressed than to share plunder with the proud."*

Pride has the attitude, "I deserve better than this! I will take matters into my own hands." When you operate out of pride, there can be no good results or long-term benefits. Better to do without than gain anything through pride, which God hates. Read Psalm 31:23 and Psalm 40:4, which also speak to the issue of pride.

January 17
Proverbs 17:20

"He whose tongue is deceitful falls into trouble."

You don't have to lie to deceive, you just have to stay silent or not tell the whole truth. Yet any time you give an impression that you think one thing while you actually believe another, you are being deceptive. Today's verse promises trouble any time you engage in this kind of verbal misdirection. You can read where deception began in Genesis 3:13 and then see a good example of it when Judas kissed Jesus while betraying Him in Luke 22:47-48.

January 18
Proverbs 18:13

"He who answers before listening - that is his folly and his shame."

It is difficult to listen and not be formulating your response while someone is still talking. What's more, you can hear their words but still not understand the full meaning of what someone says. And how well you hear others is an indication of how well you hear the Lord! Look at what Jesus had to say about how important good listening skills are in Mark 4:23-25 and consider what you can do to improve that important practice.

January 19
Proverbs 19:13

"A foolish son is his father's ruin and a quarrelsome wife is like a constant dripping."

Family can be a source of great joy or pain. Every family member should strive to apply Christian behavior first and foremost at home, and see that there is an abundance of service, encouragement, prayer and most of all, love. **Are your attitudes and behavior a blessing to your family?** Read Paul's guide for all family members in Colossians 3:18-21 and then fulfill your duty to your family with excellence and enthusiasm.

January 20
Proverbs 20:25

"It is a trap for a man to dedicate something rashly and only later to consider his vows."

It is easy to build a case that something is from the Lord because you want it to be. You can think, "**Maybe** the Lord wants me to do this ministry" or "**Perhaps** God is leading me to take that job." God doesn't deal in "maybes." He is direct and specific. **Have you ever set your course, only to find it to be a dead end?** Read how Joshua did this very thing in Joshua 9:1-18 and see how his hastiness and assumptions eventually caused Israel trouble.

January 21
Proverbs 21:31

"The horse is made ready for the day of battle, but victory rests with the Lord."

You need to develop your plans and make preparations. Just remember that when you "fight," the outcome is in God's hands. Maturity is not waiting for God to do what only you can, but also not trying to do what only God can do. **Are you waiting on God to do what He is waiting on you to do?** The apostles fishing but catching nothing in John 21:1-6 is a good real life example of this.

January 22
Proverbs 22:20-21

"Have I not written thirty sayings for you,
sayings of counsel and knowledge,
teaching you true and reliable words, so that
you can give sound answers to him who sent you."

There is power in writing. The content can be read and reviewed again and again, making it a great teaching and learning tool. **Is there writing or some other creative expression in you that you are avoiding? Of what are you afraid? How can you get started or improve?** Read the Lord's direction to the prophet in Habakkuk 2:2-4 and see if it applies to you as well.

January 23
Proverbs 23:10-11

"Do not move an ancient boundary stone
or encroach on the fields of the fatherless,
for their Defender is strong;
he will take up their case against you."

God watches out for the weak and poor. Your job is not to contribute to their problems or ignore their plight. **What are you doing for the poor and needy? Can you do more?** Be reminded of your duties in James 1:27.

January 24
Proverbs 24:14

"Know also that wisdom is sweet to your soul;
if you find it, there is a future hope for you,
and your hope will not be cut off."

If you want to be prepared for your future, then do all
you can to obtain wisdom today! And if you want to reap
good things in your future, then you must sow good
things today. **What are you doing to prepare for your
future? Are you saving, learning, doing good deeds
and growing in your ability to handle more?** Jesus
referred to this process of preparing for the future now
when He spoke the words recorded in Matthew 6:20-22.

January 25
Proverbs 25:1

"These are the proverbs of Solomon,
copied by the men of Hezekiah king of Judah."

For God's work to be completed, He must use people,
and that includes you. You can be humble and still
talk about who you are and what you can do. **Are you
willing for God to use your name and face, like
Solomon, to accomplish His purposes? Can you
surrender your desire for privacy to Him?** Jesus was
a public figure and you can read about how busy He was
in Mark 3:20-22.

January 26
Proverbs 26:24

"A malicious man disguises himself with his lips,
but in his heart he harbors deceit."

If you want to "clean up" your speech, you have to work on your heart! **What heart area, like cynicism, sarcasm or arrogance, may be affecting your speech more than you realize? What steps can you take to correct the problem?** Jesus Himself pointed out that the heart is the source when speech is a problem in Luke 6:45.

January 27
Proverbs 27:7

*"He who is full loathes honey,
but to the hungry even what is bitter tastes sweet."*

Sometimes God will allow you to go without so you can appreciate what you have and what He is about to give you, as described in Deuteronomy 8:1-18. **Do you appreciate what you have or do you take it for granted? Can you thank God for your current situation even if you are experiencing lack or an unexpected setback?**

January 28
Proverbs 28:9

*"If anyone turns a deaf ear to the law,
even his prayers are detestable."*

Prayer is no substitute for obedience. You cannot do what you choose and then pray to ask God for help. Prayer should flow out of a relationship with the Lord that includes studying and obeying God's word, which contains His revealed will. **What plan do you have in place to grow in your knowledge of God's "law"?** Jesus addressed the need for obedience in Matthew 7:21-23.

January 29
Proverbs 29:13

"The poor man and the oppressor have this in common: the Lord gives sight to the eyes of both."

There should be no class or economic distinctions in the body of Christ. Both rich and poor must remember that God is the Father of them both. Yet it is up to the privileged to reach out to those less so. **What are you doing to fellowship and befriend those of less economic means than you?** James, the brother of Jesus, spoke to this issue in James 2:1-13. Read it to better understand what today's verse is trying to convey.

January 30
Proverbs 30:20

"This is the way of an adulteress:
She eats and wipes her mouth and says,
'I've done nothing wrong.'"

It can be difficult to say, "I was wrong, forgive me." And saying, "I'm sorry," is not the same as saying, "Forgive me." It is easier to blame someone else or to explain why you did or said what you did. Yet you cannot get forgiveness unless you acknowledge what you have done to God and others. **Is it hard for you to say, "I messed up"?** Perhaps reading 1 John 1:8-10 will help you understand why this is so important.

January 31
Proverbs 31:5

"Lest they drink and forget what the law decrees,
and deprive all the oppressed of their rights."

God's word is clear: take care of the poor! It is easy, however, to be 'intoxicated' with other concerns and causes, and to forget your duty and responsibility to them. **What are you doing to help the 'have-nots' in your community and the world?** Read the word of the Lord through Isaiah to God's people concerning their lack of respect for the poor in Isaiah 10:1-3.

A DAILY
TASTE OF
PROVERBS

FEBRUARY

February 1
Proverbs 1:10-11

"Do not give in to them. If they say, 'Come along with us; let's lie in wait for someone's blood, let's waylay some harmless soul.'"

It matters who your friends are and with whom you spend time. **Are your friends helping you grow in the Lord or trying to divert your path? If your relationships aren't helping in your spiritual journey, is it time to make changes?** What you need is a friend like Jonathan was to David, and then you need to be the same kind of friend to someone else (read 1 Samuel 20).

February 2
Proverbs 2:1

"My son, if you accept my words and store up my commands within you . . ."

You should not read God's word casually, but endeavor to study and memorize it. **Do you have a Bible reading program? Are you taking any courses that will enhance your understanding? Do you spend any time memorizing His word?** Read Psalm 119:11 and 1 Thessalonians 2:13 as further exhortation to put God's word deep inside your heart and mind.

February 3
Proverbs 3:34

"He mocks proud mockers but gives grace to the humble."

In some ways, you determine how God will relate to

you. If you choose to be proud, He may oppose you. If you choose humility, He gives you grace. **So if you don't have God's grace in any area of your life, is it because pride is blocking the way?** Read the simple promise in Psalm 147:6 and then make your choice.

February 4
Proverbs 4:14

"Do not set foot on the path of the wicked or walk in the way of evil men."

Your task is pretty simple: Stay as far away from evil as possible! The most effective way to do this is to look for opportunities to do good. **What good deeds can you do today? What good words can you say today? What good thoughts can you think today?** Paul gave clear instructions to help you fulfill today's verse in Romans 12:9-21.

February 5
Proverbs 5:3-4

"For the lips of an adulteress drip honey, and her speech is smoother than oil; but in the end she is bitter as gall, sharp as a double-edged sword."

There are many voices, both external and internal, that try to entice you away from the Lord. They all promise pleasure but really only deliver pain. Jeremiah delivered a stinging rebuke to Israel and Judah that they had committed adultery by being unfaithful to the Lord and His commands. **Are you being faithful to Him or 'messing around' with other gods?** You can read what the Lord said about this in Jeremiah 3:1-5.

February 6
Proverbs 6:2

"If you have been trapped by what you said, ensnared by the words of your mouth . . ."

It is so easy to get into trouble through what you say. The easiest remedy is to watch your words carefully. The other is to ask forgiveness when you hurt or wound someone with words. The third is to keep your word, which means to make promises sparingly but to treat them as sacred when you do. **Where do you need to work on your speech and talk?** For help with your speech read Proverbs 12:18 and Proverbs 15:26.

February 7
Proverbs 7:21

"With persuasive words she led him astray; she seduced him with her smooth talk."

You must be careful whose voice you heed, even those voices in your own mind! You are always talking to yourself - it's called self-talk - and you must control your self-talk or it will control you, sometimes talking you out of doing the will of God. **How is your thinking these days? Is it vibrant and full of possibilities or are you being 'seduced' by fear and doubt?** For a good example of bad thinking, read the story of Samson and Delilah in Judges 16:1-22.

February 8
Proverbs 8:5

"You who are simple, gain prudence; you who are foolish, gain understanding."

There are no shortcuts to wisdom. First, you must want it. Then you must go where you can get it. Finally, you must pay the price to obtain it. You know you have wisdom when people seek you out to obtain some. **Are you a source of wisdom for others and yourself?** For inspiration, look at the impact of Solomon's wisdom in 1 Kings 10:1-13 and set a goal to eventually have the same affect in your own sphere of influence.

February 9
Proverbs 9:6

"Leave your simple ways and you will live;
walk in the way of understanding."

The early believers referred to the Way, a life with direction and commitment to the Lord that set them apart from all others. Their Way was distinct from all others as a life filled with prayer and generosity. **Are you walking in the Way today? What way is that Way taking you? What difference has it made in your life?** Paul himself referred to the Way as you can read in Acts 24:14.

February 10
Proverbs 10:12

"Hatred stirs up dissension,
but love covers over all wrongs."

If there is dissension, hatred can be the cause. On the other hand, love doesn't just forgive wrongs, it covers them, not to be mentioned again. This is how God treats you, lovingly covering your sins. **Are you a source of dissension or peace?** That will be determined by your ability to overlook wrongs. A great example of this is how Joseph treated Mary in Matthew 1:18-19.

February 11
Proverbs 11:20

---

*"The Lord detests men of perverse heart
but he delights in those whose ways are blameless."*

Blameless does not mean perfect. Blameless means being someone who has dealt with his or her offenses and sins, asking God and men for forgiveness. Yet those who act like they have no problems or blame are often deceived and in danger of having a perverse or wayward heart, for they lack humility. **Do you want to delight God's heart?** Then work at being blameless, which means being honest and transparent. Read what David said in Psalm 37:18 and remember that David was not perfect but he was blameless and still is today!

February 12
Proverbs 12:4

---

*"A wife of noble character is her husband's crown,
but a disgraceful wife is like decay in his bones."*

What you do affects others around you, especially family and others closest to you. In this verse, a noble wife is commended as an adornment for her husband. That means a noble church is an adornment for Christ. **How well are you relating to those closest to you? Are you a source of blessing or problems?** For New Testament insight on the family, read Ephesians 5:21-33.

February 13
Proverbs 13:14

---

*"The teaching of the wise is a fountain of life,
turning a man from the snares of death."*

It was good teaching that directed Joseph, David and Daniel when they were faced with difficult circumstances that threatened their futures. Yet each one relied on what they knew to be true and God not only delivered them, but also promoted them to important positions. **Are you in some major test of life where things look bleak?** It's not time to panic or take matters into your own hands. It's time to trust God! For a great example of this, read how David responded when he had a chance to kill his enemy Saul in 1 Samuel 24.

February 14
Proverbs 14:26

"He who fears the Lord has a secure fortress, and for his children it will be a refuge."

Some believe that if you trust the Lord, you will never suffer or be in harm's way. That is not true. You don't need a fortress unless there are powerful enemies who are trying to overwhelm you. The good news is that the Lord is a refuge and His protection extends to the children of the righteous. **Are you aware of the fact that you are in a spiritual war? Are you taking refuge where you should, or in your own strength?** See what Paul said in 2 Corinthians 10:3-6 about spiritual warfare and then fight to win the battle for your family.

February 15
Proverbs 15:9

"The Lord detests the way of the wicked but he loves those who pursue righteousness."

This verse states there is a specific path for both the wicked and the righteous, and that righteousness is something you must aggressively pursue. **What are you doing to pursue right living? What steps are you taking to insure you are on a path that God loves and of which He approves?** David spoke to the way of the righteous in Psalm 32:8-10 and also had something to say about the way of the wicked there as well.

February 16
Proverbs 16:25

"There is a way that seems right to a man but in the end it leads to death."

God wants you to use reason, but you must start from the correct assumption or else your conclusions will always be wrong! It is not good to use the word "maybe" when you are referring to God's will for your life. "Maybe I got that phone call because God wants me to go" or "Perhaps the Lord wants me to take that job" are examples of a wrong assumption that can lead to a bad decision. God is not a 'maybe' God; He makes His purpose clear. Note how David thought in 2 Samuel 4 and see that if he thought 'maybe,' he would have overlooked what the assassins had done, thinking that perhaps God had used them to promote him.

February 17
Proverbs 17:4

"A wicked man listens to evil lips; a liar pays attention to a malicious tongue."

The problem began in the Garden, when Eve and then Adam listened to the lie of the serpent. **What lie did the serpent tell?** He said that God was a liar and had not told our first parents the whole truth! His strategy hasn't changed throughout history. First he distorts the truth and then puts the blame on God for all your troubles and those of the world. **Have you paid attention to this lie that God is anything but good and just?** Read Psalm 115 and see that the lie is still being told, but the truths you need to hold onto are contained in that psalm.

February 18
Proverbs 18:5

"It's not good to be partial to the wicked or to deprive the innocent of justice."

God is concerned with justice and you should be as well, and not only when your rights are violated. What's more, you don't need to look outside your own country to find those whom you can support. **What are you doing to stand up for the poor and innocent? Is there any work or ministry situation in which you are involved that is not treating people fairly? What are you prepared to do about it?** As an example of someone who did pervert justice and to see God's immediate response, read about Ahab and Jezebel in 1 Kings 21.

February 19
Proverbs 19:9

"A false witness will not go unpunished, and he who pours out lies will perish."

A lie can achieve its purpose in the short run, but in the long-run, a liar cannot escape the long arm of God's justice. **How committed are you to telling the truth, even when you must suffer for it?** For an example of the truth in today's verse, read about Ananias and Sapphira in Acts 5:1-11.

February 20
Proverbs 20:28

---

*"Love and faithfulness keep a king safe;
through love his throne is made secure."*

God holds rulers accountable for their actions, even if they do not profess faith in Him. He established their rule and they will eventually answer to Him. The family of Herod ruled Israel at the time of Jesus, and there is an example of this accountability in Acts 12:19-24. **As a leader, or a developing one, are you mindful that you will give an account of your leadership to God?**

February 21
Proverbs 21:4

---

*"Haughty eyes and a proud heart,
the lamp of the wicked, are sin!"*

How you think determines how you "see" things. If your thinking is affected by pride, then you will see yourself as superior to others and it will affect your speech and action. Pride can be like garlic; everyone else can detect if you have eaten it but you. **Is it time to ask the Lord and others if they detect any arrogance and pride in you? Is it also time to determine if you need to repent of any prideful deeds?** A prime example of pride in the Bible is a man named Nebuchadnezzar. You can read about how God dealt with his pride in Daniel 4.

February 22
Proverbs 22:4

---

*"Humility and the fear of the Lord
bring wealth and honor and life."*

You can never go wrong when you humble yourself and do what God wants and requires. What's more, God always rewards you when you keep Him first and foremost in life! **How can you humble yourself and fear Him today?** As an example, read how Abraham humbled himself in his situation with Lot, yet see how God blessed him in Genesis 13. (It is of note that when Lot chose his land first, he chose the region of Sodom and Gomorrah! **What does that tell you about Lot?**)

February 23
Proverbs 23:12

"Apply your heart to instruction
and your ears to words of knowledge."

You learn with your heart as you remove barriers to effective listening and comprehension. You may not listen well because you are thinking of a response or question, or you are simply distracted with worry or anxiety. If you are not a good listener, you are not a good learner! **How good are your listening skills?** Read what Jesus said about listening in Luke 8:17-18 and see how it ties into today's verse.

February 24
Proverbs 24:9

"The schemes of folly are sin,
and men detest a mocker."

Schemers and mockers are selfish, trying to impose their insight and plans on everyone else. They also consider themselves more intelligent than almost anyone else. They are not team players and consequently seldom achieve anything, but always sound like experts. **Do**

you want to be a valued team player? Then learn to contribute and encourage according to your gifts and experience. This is what Barnabas did in Acts 4:36-37 and Acts 9:26-28. Compare this to Judas and his behavior in John 12:4-6.

February 25
Proverbs 25:5

"Remove the wicked from the king's presence, and his throne will be established through righteousness."

Leaders need good people around them. No leader is smart, gifted or anointed enough to get the job done. **Of whose team are you a member? Are you contributing all you can?** A great team can be found in Acts 13:1-3. **What can you learn from that team to apply to your own?**

February 26
Proverbs 26:24-25

" A malicious man disguises himself with his lips, but in his heart he harbors deceit.
Though his speech is charming, do not believe him, for seven abominations fill his heart."

Talk is cheap. **How many times have you been "taken in" by what someone convincingly said, or covered your own heart content with dishonest words?** Determine today to speak the truth to yourself and others, and allow time for those who speak well to prove that they also back up their words with action. David and Paul addressed the need for integrity in speech with one another in Psalm 55:21 and Ephesians 5:5-7.

February 27
Proverbs 27:8

"Like a bird that strays from its nest
is a man who strays from his home."

God has a 'place' or purpose for everyone that involves not only what you do but where you will do it. **Do you know your 'place' or sphere of influence? Are you working to expand your place so that you can reach and help more people?** Give some thought today to what your place and what your mission or purpose in life are. You can see how Paul did that very thing in Romans 15:22-24.

February 28
Proverbs 28:13

"He who conceals his sins does not prosper,
but whoever confesses and renounces them
finds mercy."

When you confess your sins and ask forgiveness, God is faithful to forgive. When you ask others for forgiveness, it is the first step toward reconciliation. Yet pride can cause you to blame others or deny your faults. **Is acknowledging your sins a regular part of your spiritual practices?** Read what Jesus said about forgiveness in the Lord's prayer in Matthew 6:12 and then read what John wrote in 1 John 1:8-10.

February 29
Proverbs 29:4

"By justice a king gives a country stability, but one
who is greedy for bribes tears it down."

There is great benefit when any leader or follower, whether in a family, ministry or organization, establishes consistency through predictable behavior, decisions, values and character. Yet when that same leader or follower takes shortcuts, which is what a bribe is, it is ultimately destructive to the long-term health of the team or organization of which he or she is a member. **Do the people you work or live with know which of you is going to show up on any given day? Do your moods control the people or do they liberate and empower the people?** Go ahead and read Acts 12:19-24 and see the impact an unethical leader had on his subjects.

A Daily
Taste Of
Proverbs

March

March 1
Proverbs 1:19

"Such is the end of all who go after ill-gotten gain; it takes away the lives of those who get it."

There are consequences for every choice you make. If you choose poorly, you cannot blame God for the results. If you choose wisely, you will find life and peace. **Where are you reaping the results of bad choices you have made? Can you make better choices today that will yield blessings for you and others?** For encouragement, read what Moses wrote in Numbers 14 about Joshua and Caleb who chose to trust the Lord and in return received a great inheritance and reward.

March 2
Proverbs 2:12-13

"Wisdom will save you from the ways of wicked men . . . who leave the straight paths to walk in dark ways."

You are not immune from temptation to sin. Today's verse warns that even those who are on the straight path can stray. **What precautions are you taking to insure that you stay on the straight path? What are you doing to obtain and maintain the wisdom you need for daily living?** One thing you can do is have an accurate assessment of your potential to sin, something Peter did not have in Matthew 26:33-35.

March 3
Proverbs 3:24

"When you lie down, you will not be afraid; when you lie down, your sleep will be sweet."

Fear is the great crippler, preventing you from resting in God. It keeps you mediocre and averse to risk. **What are your debilitating fears? What would you do if it wasn't for your fear of criticism, failure, ridicule or poverty**? Read what Peter quoted Isaiah 8:12 when he urged his readers not to live in fear in 1 Peter 3:13-15.

March 4
Proverbs 4:9

"She [wisdom] will set a garland of grace on your head and present you with a crown of splendor."

There is always a reward for seeking God diligently and consistently. If you persevere, you will receive royal rewards because you are a child of the King. This does not happen overnight, however, and may require years and decades of study and committed service. **Are you prepared to serve and sow, realizing your reward may not come right away?** Read Jesus' prayer for His followers in John 17 and see what encouragement you can take from that for yourself today.

March 5
Proverbs 5:7

---

*"Now then, my sons, listen to me;
do not turn aside from what I say."*

In Revelation, John heard a 'loud voice' 21 times! God is always broadcasting for any and all to hear. **Are you listening? Are you tuned to the right station, so to speak? What are you doing to keep what God has spoken before you at all times? Have you turned aside from anything He said?** Why not do a word search for the word 'loud' in Revelation or at least look at Revelation 4:1 to see one example of heaven's inescapable voice.

March 6
Proverbs 6:23

**"For these commands are a lamp,
this teaching is a light, and
the corrections of discipline are the way of life . . . ."**

God's highways are well-lit. Guidance should not be a problem for you, for if God wants you to do His will, then He *must* reveal what that will is. **If you are struggling, is the issue that you know what God wants and really don't want to do it?** That was true with Moses who, after he exhausted a list of excuses, simply told the Lord he did not want to go in Exodus 4:13-17.

March 7
Proverbs 7:24

**"Now then, my sons, listen to me;
pay attention to what I say."**

Your job is not just to be a hearer of the Word, but also a doer. Wisdom is knowing what to do with the knowledge you gain about God and His will. **Are you paying attention to what you hear and following through with appropriate action?** Read what the Bible says about this issue in Luke 9:26-27 and James 1:22-24.

March 8
Proverbs 8:33

**"Listen to my instruction and be wise;
do not ignore it."**

Many heard Jesus but did not do what He taught. That is why He often said, "He who has ears, let him hear" (Mark 4:9). Be honest: **is there any truth you have heard, but have not yet applied in your life?** This would be something like the need to be generous, but you don't give, or the importance of prayer, but you don't pray. You may want to go and read what Jesus said about listening in Mark 4:23-25 and then apply it to your life immediately.

March 9
Proverbs 9:11

"For through me [wisdom] your days will be many, and years will be added to your life."

When you do right, there are good implications for your life in general. One is that your days of effectiveness won't be cut short by unwise behavior. **Are you making the most of your time, so much so that God may give you more?** See Ephesians 5:15-17 to read what Paul had to say about this matter.

March 10
Proverbs 10:27

"The fear of the Lord adds length to life, but the years of the wicked are cut short."

There is only one way to maximize life and that is to do God's will, which is simply doing what you love and enjoy as often as possible. **Are your days spent dreading what you do, or do you attack every day with energy and enthusiasm?** Read the summary of David's life well-lived in 1 Chronicles 29:28 and then follow his example so your life can count to the max!

March 11
Proverbs 11:22

**"Like a gold ring in a pig's snout
is a beautiful woman who shows no discretion."**

God gave you your gifts and physical attributes.
**What good are they if you don't use them for His
glory?** Consider Esther and how God used her beauty
to save her people. **How can you use what you have
and who you are to further God's purpose for you in
your world?** Paul reminds us not to be proud or boastful
of what you have or can do in 1 Corinthians 4:6-7.

March 12
Proverbs 12:5

**"The plans of the righteous are just,
but the advice of the wicked is deceitful."**

Some believe that planning is not a spiritual activity. If
you know the Lord, however, you are best equipped to
plan, for He knows the future and can let you in on it!
**Are you biased against planning? Where would you
like to be in five years? Ten years? How can you get
there from where you are today?** You may want to see
David's plans from the Lord in 1 Chronicles 28:11-21
before developing your own.

March 13
Proverbs 13:18

**"He who ignores discipline comes to poverty and
shame, but whoever heeds a correction is honored."**

Accepting correction can be difficult at any age, yet

the benefits of doing so are tremendous. What's more, you may be a leader, only to be corrected by someone younger or someone with less authority than you have as others will have insight and gifts you don't have. **Are you ignoring discipline or neglecting corrective advice in your life, work or ministry?** Read Psalm 141:4-6 to see how King David viewed correction coming from a friend.

March 14
Proverbs 14:22

**"But those who plan what is good
find love and faithfulness."**

As we noted the other day, there are great benefits to planning, especially if you plan things that will bless and build up others. Some see planning as unspiritual, but Proverbs indicates otherwise. **Did you work on your plans yet? What can you see yourself doing in five or ten years that will impact the lives of others for good?** Check out Romans 2:6-8 to read more of the rewards for those who plan well.

March 15
Proverbs 15:21

---

*"Folly delights a man who lacks judgment, but
a man of understanding keeps a straight course."*

The shortest distance between two points is a straight line. That assumes, of course, that you know where you are going. **What goals are you presently pursuing? What are your plans to achieve them? Are you on course or is it time for an adjustment?** Jesus had a goal and He pursued it as you can read in Luke 9:51.

March 16
Proverbs 16:26

**"The laborer's appetite works for him;
his hunger drives him on."**

Ambition is not always wrong, and sometimes God will put you in a place of need so that you do what's in your heart without hesitation. **What is it that you want to do? What is it that you need to do?** Perhaps it's time not to be so cautious but rather to pursue your goals with urgency, without guilt or fear. For encouragement, read Paul's summary of how hard he worked under difficult circumstances in 2 Corinthians 11:21-29.

March 17
Proverbs 17:24

**"A discerning man keeps wisdom in view,
but a fool's eyes wander to the ends of the earth."**

You achieve goals by staying single-minded and focused on the main prize. **You do have goals, don't you? What can you do today that will enable you to keep them before you, along with the plans necessary to make them happen? Perhaps a journal would be helpful or a time-management system?** You can read about your need for focus in 2 Corinthians 11:2-3.

March 18
Proverbs 18:9

**"One who is slack in his work
is brother to one who destroys."**

When you don't do something in your heart, something

is lost, the same kind of loss as if you did it and someone then destroyed it. **What have you talked about doing 'one day'? Is this the day you start or finish it? Are you maintaining your world or expanding it according to God's will for you?** See how the people followed through on David's plans from the Lord in 1 Chronicles 29:1-25 and then determine to be as diligent with your plans as they were.

March 19
Proverbs 19:15

"Laziness brings on deep sleep,
and the shiftless man goes hungry."

The eight-hour work day is a modern invention. The Lord's pattern is working six days, sunrise to sunset, and then resting on the seventh. **Are your work habits what they need to be to be productive for Him? Is your lack of energy due to lack of goals and purpose?** Read about Paul's view of hard work in 1 Corinthians 15:10 and 1 Thessalonians 5:12-14.

March 20
Proverbs 20:5

"The purposes of a man's heart are deep waters,
but a man of understanding draws them out."

At times, it is hard for you to isolate and verbalize your deepest thoughts and plans. You may not like to talk about yourself or you may not be able to see what others see in you. **Do you have coaches or mentors who are helping you draw out those plans hidden deep in your heart?** You may also want to read what Barnabas did for Paul in Acts 11:22-26.

March 21
Proverbs 21:16

"A man who strays from the path of understanding comes to rest in the company of the dead."

You make choices every day and they have implications for your future. Make good choices and you will prosper; make poor ones and you will not. You can make good choices when you follow the commands and principles in God's word. **What good choices can you make today that will bear fruit far into the future?** For help, pray the prayer of David in Psalm 25:5.

March 22
Proverbs 22:6

"Train a child in the way he should go, and when he is old he will not turn from it."

Whether parent, teacher, family or friend, you are obligated to help train the children in your life in the ways of God. **Into what youth are you investing yourself? If you are a grown child, are you true to the ways in which you were trained and raised?** If not, it's time to get back on track! Read what Paul said about raising godly children in Ephesians 6:4 and Colossians 3:21.

March 23
Proverbs 23:21

" . . . for drunkards and gluttons become poor, and drowsiness clothes them in rags."

You have a purpose and fulfilling it should cause you to be in training, so to speak. **Is your lifestyle such**

that you have energy to be productive, or are you addicted to food, drink, television, sleep, the Internet or cheap novels? Perhaps it is time for change, for if you want what you don't have, you must begin doing what you have never done. Paul spoke about purposeful discipline is in 1 Corinthians 9:27 and 2 Timothy 2:2-7.

March 24
Proverbs 24:1-2

"Do not envy wicked men,
do not desire their company;
for their hearts plot violence,
and their lips talk about making trouble."

It matters who your friends are and with whom you spend your time. **Do you have people in your life who are helping you fulfill your purpose or people who are draining you of life and energy?** Maybe it's time to reassess the company you keep (even family). Paul's principle to us regarding this in 1 Corinthians 15:33-34.

March 25
Proverbs 25:27

"It is not good to eat too much honey,
nor is it honorable to seek one's own honor."

Honor is in God's hands and He shares it with whom He wishes. A promotion or accolades are under His control, so **why fret when you are overlooked or passed over?** When the time is right, He will honor you - and God knows how to do it well. Therefore, stay faithful and steadfast, and leave the rest to Him! To reinforce this concept, read Psalm 75 and then look in Esther 6 to see how God honored Mordecai after he had been faithful.

March 26
Proverbs 26:14

"As a door turns on its hinges,
so a sluggard turns on his bed."

What are you living for? Your next meal? Your next holiday? The weekend? Don't waste or wish your life away one day at a time. Find something that gives you energy and you can do with enthusiasm, and stop 'sleep walking' your way through life! Paul had divine energy or power when he worked (see Ephesians 3:7). **How can you have this same kind of energy and power?**

March 27
Proverbs 27:12

"The prudent see danger and take refuge,
but the simple keep going and suffer for it."

Discernment is an important skill in work and life. Knowing when to proceed and when to wait requires you to watch, listen and be ready to move quickly or not at all. Most people tend to emphasize one or the other (wait or go). **What can you do to be more prudent in your relationships and decisions? Are you delaying or rushing an important decision or action?** Read what David did to develop his prudence and discernment in 1 Chronicles 14:8-17.

March 28
Proverbs 28:12

"When the righteous triumph, there is great elation;
but when the wicked rise to power,
men go into hiding."

Bad leadership causes gifted people to go into hiding, taking their skills and creativity with them. **What kind of leader are you? Do you even want to be a leader? Will people give their best for you? How can you develop as an effective leader? If you are a follower, have you 'checked out' due to a poor leader?** Take some time to read about Nehemiah's leadership skills and see what you can learn to get the kind of results he got in Nehemiah 6:15-16.

March 29
Proverbs 29:2

"When the righteous thrive, the people rejoice; when the wicked rule, the people groan."

King David learned more about leadership from Saul than anyone else - he learned how *not* to lead. **What are you learning from your leaders, both good and bad, that will shape your own leadership philosophy? Are you consciously applying that to your life, family, work and ministry?** Review Paul's requirements for being an elder in Titus 1:6-9 and see how many of those traits you can incorporate into your own character, whether you are a parent, corporate executive or pastor!

March 30
Proverbs 30:32

"If you have played the fool and exalted yourself, or if you have planned evil, clap your hand over your mouth!"

Where your job, future and promotion are involved, can you trust Him, or have you taken matters into your own hands? You can and must prepare for success, but your path to that success is in His hands. **Can you trust the Lord for your future?** You may want to read the words that have encouraged so many about planning for the future in Jeremiah 29:10-14.

March 31
Proverbs 31:4

"It is not for kings, O Lemuel – not for kings to drink wine, not for rulers to crave beer."

Leaders do not exist to serve their own needs and desires but to serve the highest priority needs of others. What's more, leaders must not be intoxicated with power or their own importance. **What kind of leader are you? What kind do you want to be?** Pharaoh, Nebuchadnezzar and Herod are examples of poor leaders; Joseph, Joshua and David are examples of good ones. For an explanation of what makes a good leader, read what Paul had to say about Timothy in Philippians 2:19-23.

A Daily Taste Of Proverbs

April

April 1
Proverbs 1:30-31

*"Since they would not accept my advice
and spurned my rebuke,
they will eat the fruit of their ways."*

Someone once said a fanatic is a person who redoubles her efforts when she has lost her way! It can be difficult to say, "I need help!" If you don't, you risk making the same mistakes over and over again. **In what area of life can you use advice? Why aren't you seeking it?** For a good example of someone who received and followed advice and rebuke read Esther 2:10 and Esther 4:12-14.

April 2
Proverbs 2:11

*"Discretion will protect you,
and understanding will guard you."*

You have many enemies as you seek to serve God and fulfill your purpose, not the least of which can be your own heart and thinking. You need to protect yourself from yourself, which is why you study, learn and grow in wisdom, knowledge, and grace. **What are you doing to secure this kind of protection?** Read what Paul had to say about your thinking in 1 Corinthians 14:20 and Ephesians 4:17.

April 3
Proverbs 3:3

*"Let love and faithfulness never leave you;
bind them around your neck,
write them on the tablet of your heart."*

How to serve the Lord is not difficult to understand; it may just be difficult to do. While you serve the Lord, He often requires that you serve other people, and they can be ungrateful, needy and demanding. **How well are you translating your love for and faith in God into practical service?** You can read 1 John 3:11-18 to learn more of what love and faithfulness require in daily life.

April 4
Proverbs 4:16

"For they cannot sleep till they do evil; they are robbed of slumber till they make someone fall."

Everyone loses sleep from time to time. It's important that you lose it for the right reasons. Some lose sleep over worry, stress, or plotting things not pleasing to the Lord. Others lose it to pray, sit with someone in need, or carry out God's will. **Why do you lose sleep?** The issue of rest is addressed in Psalm 121 and Hebrews 4:1-11.

April 5
Proverbs 5:2

"That you may maintain discretion and your lips may preserve knowledge."

It is common decency to make commitments to the Lord when things are bad, making vows of changes you will make. Yet when the pressure is off or more pressure comes, it is easy to forsake those promises. **Are you maintaining and preserving the lessons and changes that come from hard times?** For a graphic picture of this tendency, read the parable of the sower in Matthew 13:1-23 and see into which category you fall as you maintain what the Lord is doing in your life.

April 6
Proverbs 6:16

---

*"There are six things the Lord hates,
seven that are detestable to him."*

It should be your goal in life to please the Lord. You only know of what God approves or disapproves as you study His Word. **Perhaps you should also read verses 17-19 to find out what He hates and see if you are involved in any of those activities?**

April 7
Proverbs 7:7

"I saw among the simple, I noticed among the young men, a youth who lacked judgment."

It is possible to pass through life and not notice those around you. Yet every day you come in contact with people who have needs, are depressed, despairing or downtrodden. What's more, their current path is leading them to destruction. Ask the Lord to open your eyes to see those around you who need who you are and what you have. This is what Peter and John did in Acts 3:1-10.

April 8
Proverbs 8:9

---

*"To the discerning all of them are right;
they are faultless to those who have knowledge."*

Discernment and knowledge don't just happen. They require work on your part, along with some trial and error. **Are you relying on the Spirit to do for you what only you can do?** He cannot read, study or pray for you; you must do that yourself. **Are you paying the price for spiritual growth? Do you have people in your life helping you to grow and mature?** You can read more on how important this is in Ephesians 4:11-24.

April 9
Proverbs 9:4

"'Let all who are simple come in here!'
she [wisdom] says to those who lack judgment."

If you need wisdom, you must only ask and God will send it. **Why would you ask for it and God *not* send it?** Therefore you must trust that what comes after you pray is the answer you seek. Don't put faith in your ability to hear the Lord; put it in His ability to communicate with you! The process is further explained in James 1:2-8.

April 10
Proverbs 10:13

"Wisdom is found on the lips of the discerning,
but a rod is for the back of him who lacks judgment."

When you lack wisdom, it can be painful as you experience the consequences of your bad choices. When you have it, people seek you out to get it. **Which would you rather be: a fountain of good advice or a good example of how not to live?** This comes down to reaping what you sow, which is described in Haggai 1.

April 11
Proverbs 11:12

"A man who lacks judgment derides his neighbor,
but a man of understanding holds his tongue."

It is all too easy to talk badly about people when they aren't present. It is much more difficult to talk to them directly about a problem you are having with them. **Is it time you hold your tongue where other people are concerned, unless it is to say something good? Do you need to confront someone about a situation you are carrying in your heart?** The psalmist addresses this problem in Psalm 12 and Psalm 15:1-4.

April 12
Proverbs 12:23

"A prudent man keeps his knowledge to himself, but the heart of fools blurts out folly."

It can be difficult to be silent when you know something and others aren't asking for your opinion or input. It's even worse when you have nothing to say - and still say it. **Do you need to improve your listening skills and learn to keep quiet?** Check out what James wrote about the tongue in James 3:3-6.

April 13
Proverbs 13:16

"Every prudent man acts out of knowledge, but a fool exposes his folly."

If you want to go where you have never been, you must do what you have never done. You can only act out of what you know, so to do new things, you must think new thoughts based on new knowledge and awareness. **What are you doing to improve yourself so that your knowledge base can grow?** See the result of those who reject knowledge in Romans 1:28-29 and the kind of knowledge you need to have in Colossians 3:9-10.

April 14
Proverbs 14:29

"A patient man has great understanding,
but a quick-tempered man displays folly."

Anger is a legitimate emotion, just like joy or sorrow. It is not wrong in and of itself unless it motivates you to engage in wrong behavior. Patience is a virtue that can help you control and direct your anger toward positive expressions. **What rules your life: patience or anger?** A good motto or guideline for anger-free living is found in Romans 12:12.

April 15
Proverbs 15:14

"The discerning heart seeks knowledge,
but the mouth of a fool feeds on folly."

If you don't learn interesting things, you won't have any interesting things to talk or write or paint! You don't gain knowledge by being passive. You must work to obtain it, and the more you seek, the more you will find. **What are you doing to gain it? Do you have a reading program? Are you taking classes or attending seminars? Do you meet the expectations that Paul had for believers on this issue in Romans 15:14?**

April 16
Proverbs 16:21

"The wise in heart are called discerning,
and pleasant words promote instruction."

You probably teach others more often than you realize,

whether they are your peers, children, friends, family or fellow workers. Knowing what to say *and* how to say it enhances your ability to get your message across. **Do others like to be around you or seek you out for advice? Are you known for your positive, encouraging words?** Jesus not only said the right thing but also said it in the right way according to Isaiah 50:4-5 and Luke 4:22.

April 17
Proverbs 17:18

"A man lacking in judgment strikes hands in pledge and puts up security for his neighbor."

You cannot want something for others more than they do, or 'co-sign' for their problem when they are not willing to take responsibility. **Are you losing sleep for people who aren't losing sleep over their own situation?** Perhaps it's time to let go of their problem and pay attention to your own issues! **Do you think this is the meaning of what Jesus said in Matthew 10:37?**

April 18
Proverbs 18:12

"Before his downfall a man's heart is proud, but humility comes before honor."

Are you going through a season of humility? That's a good thing, for honor is sure to follow. Yet if you don't humble yourself, God may humble or even humiliate you. The choice is yours but, whatever you do, don't allow pride to get the upper hand in your life. Read how God feels about pride at Luke 1:51, 1 Corinthians 13:4 and 1 John 2:16.

April 19
Proverbs 19:25

---

*". . . rebuke a discerning man,
and he will gain knowledge."*

All of us are smarter than one of us, which means you cannot learn in isolation. You need others not just to rebuke you when you are doing wrong, but also when you are not doing the purposeful things you need to do. **Who is close enough to you to rebuke you? Do you make it easy for them to give you input? Do you listen? Is there anything you can learn from how Paul rebuked Peter at Galatians 2:11-14?**

April 20
Proverbs 20:12

---

*"Ears that hear and eyes that see –
the Lord has made them both."*

Many saw and heard Jesus, but were unchanged by His presence. You must work to overcome the spiritual dullness that so easily entangles your senses. **Do you take time to think, pray, reflect and listen? Do you have a journal to help you remember what God has shown you?** For help with your spiritual focus, heed Hebrews 12:1-2 for seeing and Luke 8:18 for listening.

April 21
Proverbs 21:20

"In the house of the wise are stores of choice food and oil, but a foolish man devours all he has."

The wise always have something to give to others. Fools

consume what they have on themselves. **Do you waste your creative energies on worry and anxiety? Are you always in 'receive' mode when you should be in 'give'? What steps can you take to stop consuming what God gives you? What do you think Paul meant when he wrote that God will make you "rich in every way" in 2 Corinthians 9:11?**

April 22
Proverbs 22:12

"The eyes of the Lord keep watch over knowledge, but he frustrates the words of the unfaithful."

God is active, keeping watch over or frustrating people according to their degree of faithfulness. **If you are frustrated right now, could it be a result of your own unfaithfulness to pray, give or bless others? Are you being your own biggest hindrance where receiving God's help is concerned?** Check out Proverbs 19:3 to understand more of what today's verse is saying to you.

April 23
Proverbs 23:1

"When you sit down to dine with a ruler, note well what is before you."

There are two types of leaders: those who take and those who give. You should not assume all leaders are one or the other, but should consider their values before you decide to follow. Once you decide to follow, you should submit to and cooperate with their leadership. **Are you a godly follower? How do you know one way or the other?** You can find a good example of a godly follower in 1 Samuel 14:1-14.

April 24
Proverbs 24:32

*"I applied my heart to what I observed
and learned a lesson from what I saw . . . ."*

If you don't pay attention, you will miss things that
are happening right before your eyes. When you are
distracted with worry, pride, or selfishness, you easily
miss someone's body language and their unspoken
messages to you. **Do you pay attention or are you
distracted or absorbed in your own world?** As a good
example, look at Jesus' ability to observe others when
He watched people giving their offerings in Mark 2:5-12.

April 25
Proverbs 25:7-8

*"What you have seen with your eyes do not bring
hastily to court, for what will you do in the end if
your neighbor puts you to shame?"*

**How often have you jumped to conclusions before
getting all the information? How often have you
fretted over something you thought would happen
but didn't?** You must learn to observe but not jump to
conclusions until you have all the information. When you
have it, you need to trust in the Lord and not fret. An
example of people who jumped to the wrong conclusion
based on what they saw is in Joshua 22:10-34.

April 26
Proverbs 26:16

*"The sluggard is wiser in his own eyes
than seven men who answer discreetly."*

Have you ever noticed how creative you can be to come up with excuses for why you are not doing something you need to do? Most laziness is rooted in some kind of fear, but you 'spin' that fear into something that sounds better. **What are your favorite excuses? What can you do to overcome them?** You must walk in the works God has prepared for you to do, as Paul stated in Ephesians 2:8-10.

April 27
Proverbs 27:17

"As iron sharpens iron,
so one man sharpens another."

You need people in your life who will challenge and help you grow. That means they may not always tell you what you want to hear, but what you need to hear. **Do you have these people in your life? Who are they and how can you draw even more from them? Do you play that role for someone else?** As a good example of this, read how Paul sharpened a man named Philemon in a short epistle by the same name.

April 28
Proverbs 28:20

"A faithful man will be richly blessed,
but one eager to get rich will not go unpunished."

There are no shortcuts to God's blessings, and faithfulness is a key. What's more, there are ways for God to bless you beyond finances. **Do you desire to be rich or blessed? Can you be content with what you have and not wait for more before reaching out to others?** Jesus spoke about this in Luke 16:1-9.

April 29
Proverbs 29:11

***"A fool gives full vent to his anger,
but a wise man keeps himself under control."***

Notice this verse does not say that anger is wrong, but acting out of anger is foolish. If you direct your anger toward action to correct a wrong, attitude or habit, then you are wise. If you just bluster and blow with no redemptive or corrective action, then you are indeed a fool. **What role does anger play in your life at present?** In Mark 3:1-5 and Mark 11:15-17, Jesus was angry yet did not sin, which indicates it is possible to use anger as motivation to do good and not harm or destroy.

April 30
Proverbs 30:15

"The leech has two daughters. 'Give, give!' they cry."

A mature person is one who gives more than he or she takes. A leech is a taker, one who literally sucks the life out of another. **Are you a taker or a giver? A whiner or encourager? A builder of people or a user of people? What can you do to bless those around you today?** You can read about a "leech" in 2 Kings 5:15-27.

A DAILY
TASTE OF
PROVERBS

MAY

May 1
Proverbs 1:5

"Let the wise listen and add to their learning, and let the discerning get guidance."

God wants you to know and do His will, so guidance should not be a problem for the believer. What's more, your experience should add to your knowledge and discernment as you learn from mistakes and successes. **Are you growing or have you plateaued in your walk and life? What can you do to regain momentum?** You can read about someone who wrestled with life and consequently added to his learning in Ecclesiastes 2.

May 2
Proverbs 2:5

"Then you will understand the fear of the Lord, and find the knowledge of God."

God promises that if you seek Him you will find Him. This cannot, however, be a passive or lukewarm pursuit. **Are you seeking the Lord with consistency and fervor? Why are you seeking Him? What questions are you asking Him? What are you doing with the answers?** As an example of how to seek Him, read Psalm 63.

May 3
Proverbs 3:1

"My son, do not forget my teaching, but keep my commands in your heart."

Keeping God's commands in your heart takes effort. It requires that you read, study, and meditate on His word regularly. **How are your reading and study habits where God's word is concerned? Are you putting the time and effort in to be able to apply His word to your own life and the lives of others?** When you do, you can be confident that God will help you in the process, as described in Jeremiah 31:31-34.

May 4
Proverbs 4:23

"Above all else, guard your heart,
for it is the wellsprings of life."

This verse warns you to guard your heart, for there are things that will assail it to poison your source of life. **In what condition is your heart? Free from bitterness and anger? Full of joy and gratitude? What are you doing to guard it so that you can enjoy the fullness of life the Lord intends for you?** Read John 7:37-38 and Joel 2:12-13 to get more insight into the importance and power of heart maintenance.

May 5
Proverbs 5:11

"At the end of your life you will groan,
when your flesh and body are spent."

You are a spiritual being having a temporary human experience. That's why Jesus said to lay up treasures in heaven where moth and rust can't ruin what you do. **Is your main focus this life or the next? Are you sending your time and money ahead to your heavenly account?** You can read what Jesus had to say about this matter in Luke 16:9, Peter in 1 Peter 1:3-4 and Paul in Colossians 1:3-6.

May 6
Proverbs 6:5

"Free yourself, like a gazelle from the hand of the hunter, like a bird from the snare of the fowler."

Whatever has you enslaved is your god. It can be shopping, television, food, nicotine, sex, drugs, alcohol or the Internet. **Are you ready to free yourself with God's help?** Paul consistently wrote that he was a slave or bond-servant of Christ. **Are you able to say the same thing?** Read 2 Peter 2:19, Romans 1:1 and Titus 1:1 and do what you must to follow Paul's example.

May 7
Proverbs 7:15

"I came out to meet you;
I looked for you and have found you!"

Temptation is always looking for you and sometimes it finds a willing partner! One way to avoid it is to be doing good when it finds you! Another way is to run away as fast as you can. Sometimes the temptation is to do something wrong; other times it is *not* to do something good. **What are your common temptations and how do you best handle them?** For help with temptation, read 1 Corinthians 10:13 and apply its truth.

May 8
Proverbs 8:31

"Rejoicing in his whole world
and delighting in mankind."

God doesn't just tolerate you, He delights in you. He is

often more comfortable with who you are than you! It is His good pleasure to give you good things so that you will rejoice in Him. **Are you rejoicing? Can you receive His love? Or are you spending time trying to change things about yourself that He is not directing you to change?** You may want to read more about God's love in Zephaniah 3:17, John 3:16 and 1 John 3:1.

May 9
Proverbs 9:18

"Little do they know that the dead are there, that her guests are in the depths of the grave."

You embrace some activities because they give you life and joy. Others take life and energy from you because they are not part of what God has for you to do. **Do you wake up looking forward to your day or dreading it? If the latter, do you think that is how God wants you to live?** The Lord urges you to choose life in Deuteronomy 30:19-20 and tells you how to do just that.

May 10
Proverbs 10:4

"Lazy hands make a man poor, but diligent hands bring wealth."

This verse presents two work options: laziness and diligence. The former does just enough to get by; the latter fills time with productive activities. What's more, the diligent do 'right things' *and* do 'things right,' which lead to promotions and financial reward. **If you have lack now, could your work habits be the problem?** To see what Paul said about work habits, read Ephesians 4:28, Colossians 3:22-24 and 1 Thessalonians 4:11-12.

May 11
Proverbs 11:5

"The righteousness of the blameless makes a straight way for them, but the wicked are brought down by their own wickedness."

Guidance should never be a problem for the righteous. God makes His way for you clear, but resists the path of the wicked. **That being true, where do you see yourself in three years? Five years? Ten years?** For added insight into this concept, read these six verses in Psalm 119:32, 35, 101, 104, 105 and 128.

May 12
Proverbs 12:21

"No harm befalls the righteous, but the wicked have their fill of trouble."

This verse does not mean the righteous never have any struggles, rather that their struggles are not due to their wicked deeds. God uses their struggles to build character, while the trouble of the wicked is to judge sin and lead to repentance. **Are you rejoicing in your trials, knowing that God is in control of your life?** If you are going through tough times and wonder why the wicked are not, read Psalm 94 to be encouraged today.

May 13
Proverbs 13:17

"A wicked messenger falls into trouble, but a trustworthy envoy brings healing."

You have been entrusted with a message of the good

news of the gospel. **Are you being a faithful envoy with that message? With whom do you share that good news? How often? What are you doing to support other faithful envoys in the field?** To see this verse in action go read Luke 9:1-6.

May 14
Proverbs 14:14

"The faithless will be fully repaid for their ways, and the good man rewarded for his."

Examine your personal habits to determine if your lack of faithfulness is the source of your current situation. **Is it possible to lack because you have not sown? If you have no friends, is it because you have not been friendly? If you lack finances, is it because you have not given?** Read what the wisdom teacher had to say about giving in Ecclesiastes 11:1-6 and then apply his truth to every area of your life.

May 15
Proverbs 15:6

"The house of the righteous contains great treasure, but the income of the wicked brings them trouble."

Your home should be a refuge for your family and for others. Don't underestimate the healing power a godly household contains. **Do you practice hospitality, opening your home to short or long-term guests? What can you do to make your house a source of joy and healing for many?** Both Hebrews 13:2 and 1 Peter 4:9 speak to the issue of hospitality. **Are you living up to those verses?**

May 16
Proverbs 16:32

"Better a patient man than a warrior, a man who controls his temper than one who takes a city."

It is interesting that God considers a person strong when they control their strength, not when they express it. **How patient have you been lately? What situation seems the hardest for you to deal with where patience is concerned? Is it people or circumstances that affect you the most?** Read what Paul said about applying patience with others in 1 Thessalonians 5:14.

May 17
Proverbs 17:27

"A man of knowledge uses words with restraint, and a man of understanding is even-tempered."

Just because you know doesn't mean you have to let people know you know. Your words should count when you speak and not just used to vent opinions and grievances. **Are you making your words count these days? Are your words angry or gracious?** Read what Peter had to say about this in 1 Peter 4:11.

May 18
Proverbs 18:1

"A man who isolates himself seeks his own desire, he rages against all wise judgment."

There is nothing wrong with being introverted, but being a loner is a willful and rebellious act. **Where and why have you cut yourself off from other people, those**

who have what you need and complement who you are? What can you do to reconnect? Read about the blessing that comes from being with others in Psalm 133 and remember that Jesus promised to be present where two or three gather in His name (see Matthew 18:20).

May 19
Proverbs 19:3

"A man's own folly ruins his life,
yet his heart rages against the Lord."

It is important that you take personal responsibility for your life choices and consequences. **Is there any life disappointment for which you hold God responsible, when it may have been your own bad decisions that caused the problem? Is there any area of your life where you believe a lie and consider God less than good and faithful?** Read how Job responded to his calamities in Job 1:20-22 and Job 2:8-10 and see what you can learn.

May 20
Proverbs 20:21

"An inheritance quickly gained at the beginning
will not be blessed at the end."

You must develop your ability to enjoy and handle success. **What is your personal development plan? Do you want more or are you content with what you have? What would a good 'inheritance' be for you? In other words, how would you define success in your life five, ten or fifteen years from now?** As an example of one who patiently waited for his inheritance, read about Caleb in Joshua 14:6-15.

May 21
Proverbs 21:1

"The king's heart is in the hand of the Lord; he directs it like a watercourse wherever he pleases."

God works through leadership, both those who know Him and those who don't. **Is your focus on the leaders you can see or the God you cannot see?** Don't ever give leaders the honor that is only due to God, but don't be rebellious and arrogant either. Read what Paul wrote about how to relate to authorities in Romans 13:1-7.

May 22
Proverbs 22:29

"Do you see a man skilled in his work? He will serve before kings; he will not stand before obscure men."

God does not promote potential, but promotes and uses those who have developed their potential. **What steps are you willing to take to be the best 'you' possible? Will it involve school, reading, challenging work or lessons? What will it cost you to develop you?** Paul stood before kings because of his preparation as you can read in Acts 25:23-27.

May 23
Proverbs 23:23

"Buy truth and do not sell it;
get wisdom, discipline and understanding."

It seems that the higher the price you pay for truth, the less likely you are to sell or give it away. That explains why you must go through hard times for success - to make it more valuable in the long run. **What price are you willing to pay to get wisdom and insight?** Read what Jesus had to say to one of the churches in Revelation about what you need to buy from Him in Revelation 3:17-19.

May 24
Proverbs 24:10

"If you falter in times of trouble,
how small is your strength."

Adversity is part of everyone's life, especially the believer, for it builds and manifests your strength. It is important that you allow the adversity to accomplish its purpose and not cut it short or oppose its purpose. **How are you dealing with any adversity these days? Are you thankful and joyous in the midst of it?** Read how Paul encouraged one church that endured suffering in 2 Thessalonians 1:4-11 and see if you can learn anything from his words to them.

May 25
Proverbs 25:2

"It is the glory of God to conceal a matter;
to search out a matter is the glory of kings."

God 'hides' things so you will seek Him for clarity and answers. This seeking cannot be passive, but must involve active asking, listening and journaling. **Are you seeking Him for answers and direction right now?** Don't give up until you have what you need. Read what David said about seeking the Lord in a time of need in Psalm 27 and be encouraged to seek with all your heart as you search out answers for your life and purpose.

May 26
Proverbs 26:4-5

"Do not answer a fool according to his folly,
or you will be just like him yourself.
Answer a fool according to his folly,
or he will be wise in his own eyes."

To answer or not to answer? Some people are ready to hear what you have to say and others aren't. You must rely on God's guidance to know what to say and when to say it to whoever may be ready to hear. **How receptive are you to those with whom you speak?** To see how Jesus handled this challenge, read John 12:48-50.

May 27
Proverbs 27:2

"Let another praise you, and not your own mouth;
someone else, and not your own lips."

God can do great things through people who don't mind if others get the credit. **Are you willing to see your ideas and work used for the good of others without them knowing you were the source of the blessing?** At the same time, the verse says to allow someone else to praise you. **How easy is it for you to wait for others to honor you?** To see how someone answered both those questions, check out the story of Haman in Esther 2:19-23 and Esther 6.

May 28
Proverbs 28:26

"He who trusts in himself is a fool,
but he walks in wisdom is kept safe."

It is common to underestimate your potential and the power of your ideas. That's why you need other people speaking into your life if you are to walk in wisdom. **Who are your coaches and mentors? Who challenges and broadens your perspective on life and purpose? Who is on your personal 'board of directors'?** As an example of the kind of input and encouragement you need from others, read about the encounter that Jonathan and David had in 1 Samuel 23:16-18.

May 29
Proverbs 29:20

"Do you see a man who speaks in haste?
There is more hope for a fool than for him."

How often have you rushed to judgment, upset over something that can happen but seldom does? You fuss and worry, only to expend a lot of energy over nothing. Confront and correct this pessimistic tendency or you will soon find a problem in every situation, leaving you a victim of your surging emotions and anger. As an example of someone who almost lost his healing due to this tendency, read Naaman's story in 2 Kings 5:1-15.

May 30
Proverbs 30:5

"Every word of God is flawless;
he is a shield to those who take refuge in Him."

The Lord makes Himself known and present in your life through His Word. Therefore, His Word is your lifeline and support. **How much time are you spending reading, studying and memorizing His Word? What more can you do? Is He truly your shield and do you**

take total refuge in Him in times of trouble? Read what the psalmist said about the Lord and His Word in Psalm 119:113-115 and then renew your efforts to make God's Word your source of help, comfort and guidance.

May 31
Proverbs 31:1

"The sayings of King Lemuel –
an oracle his mother taught him."

Wisdom is best imparted in a family setting and is usually not appreciated until children are older. **Are you applying the good advice your parents imparted to you as a child? If you are a parent, are you regularly teaching this same kind of wisdom, even if your children complain or seem to reject it?** Teaching the next generation was part of God's command to Israel as you can read in Deuteronomy 4:9-10.

A Daily
Taste Of
Proverbs

June

June 1
Proverbs 1:32

*"For the waywardness of the simple will kill them,
and the complacency of fools destroy them."*

Setting bold goals for personal growth is important
for your success in the Lord. **What is your "elegant
dream" for your life? What goals do you need to set
to fulfill that dream? What do you see yourself doing
five, ten or twenty years from now? What can you do
today to prepare for your vision of tomorrow?** Paul
had very precise bold goals, which were expressed in
part in Romans 15:20-21.

June 2
Proverbs 2:4

*"And if you look for it [wisdom] as for silver
and search for it [wisdom] as for hidden treasure."*

**If you had a guarantee there was treasure buried on
your property, how long and hard would you look
for it?** You have that promise concerning the treasure of
wisdom in God's word for your life and the situations you
face. **How hard and long are you willing to search
and seek?** Read what Jesus had to say about paying
the price for wisdom in Matthew 13:44-46.

June 3
Proverbs 3:9-10

*"Honor the Lord with your wealth,
with the firstfruits of all your crops;
then your barns will be filled to overflowing,
and your vats will brim over with new wine."*

One of the best means to determine your trust level in God is your giving. **Is your current lack due to your stinginess? Would God say you are a generous person? Would others? Do you find it easy to trust the Lord where money is concerned?** You can read what Paul had to say to the Corinthian church about giving in 2 Corinthians 8:1-15.

June 4
Proverbs 4:18

"The path of the righteous is like the first gleam of dawn, shining ever brighter till the full light of day."

Your path should be bright because you choose to walk in the light of His word. Therefore guidance should not be a challenge because God *wants* you to know and do His will. This is further explained by Psalm 119:105: "Your word is a lamp to my feet and a light for my path." **How bright is the light in your life?** John wrote about walking in the light in John 1:1-9.

June 5
Proverbs 5:3

"For the lips of an adulteress drip honey, and her speech is smoother than oil."

There are many causes, philosophies, political worldviews and people who try to beguile you with convincing arguments that are contrary to God and His Word. Don't be taken in by their appeals. Be true to Him. **Can you identify any area of life where you have become friends with the world and thus an opponent of God?** James was concerned with this same issue and wrote about it in James 4:4-5.

June 6
Proverbs 6:6

"Go to the ant, you sluggard;
consider its ways and be wise!"

The ant's work ethic is legendary. **Is yours?** There is no substitute for hard work in an area you enjoy. **Do you look forward to your work or dread it?** The Bible has much to say about hard work, starting in Genesis 1:28 and continuing through Ecclesiastes 5:18, Acts 20:34 and on to 1 Thessalonians 2:9.

June 7
Proverbs 7:3

"Bind them [God's commands] on your fingers;
write them on the tablet of your heart."

There are many ways to assimilate God's commands, such as memorizing verses, reading the Word, journaling, preaching or teaching, listening to a version of the recorded Word, reading a devotional or even writing one! **What works best for you so that God's Word can be written on your heart's tablets?** To reinforce this truth, read Ezekiel 11:18-20 and Psalm 119:10-12 in light of today's topic.

June 8
Proverbs 8:1

"Does not wisdom call out?
Does not understanding raise her voice?"

Wisdom is always broadcasting. **Are you tuned to her channel? She is speaking, but are you listening?**

And what are you doing to record and remember what she says? It is important that you put your faith not in your ability to hear God's voice but in His ability to 'speak' to you & answer your prayer for help. To reinforce this, the book of Revelation states that heaven spoke to John in a *loud* voice 21 times! (See Revelation 1:10 and 5:12 for just two examples.)

June 9
Proverbs 9:2

"If you are wise, your wisdom will reward you. If you are a mocker, you alone will suffer."

It is in your best interests to seek wisdom about your life's work and decisions. If you mock or scorn wisdom, you will suffer by continually making bad decisions, for which you and others will suffer. **If you asked others, would they say you are wise or do you ignore those who carry the wisdom you need?** You can see that God's wisdom was mocked by sinful men in Psalm 89:50-51 and Matthew 27:29-41. Make sure you are not numbered among those who do the same.

June 10
Proverbs 10:19

"When words are many, sin is not absent, but he who holds his tongue is wise."

Do you sometimes talk too much? At times do you regret what you said, especially to those closest to you? It is not necessary to speak your mind on every occasion. Determine to be a better listener and use words to encourage and not to attack or show off. James spoke about your tongue and speech in James 3:5-10.

June 11
Proverbs 11:31

---

*"If the righteous receive their due on earth,
how much more the ungodly and the sinner."*

God is faithful to reward those who are diligent to do
good deeds. It may seem like He has forgotten but He
has not. **Have you despaired of God's desire to bless
you?** Just keep on doing what you know is right for He is
watching. Passages that reinforce today's message are
Matthew 10:40-42, Mark 10:29-31 and Psalm 73.

June 12
Proverbs 12:3

---

*"A man cannot be established through wickedness,
but the righteous cannot be uprooted."*

There are some who try to establish themselves and put
confidence in their own abilities. They are trying to do
the impossible. Others put their trust in Him and cannot
be moved because God watches over them. **To which
group do you belong?** To look at more on this issue,
read Jeremiah 9:23-24 and the short book of Nahum.

June 13
Proverbs 13:1

---

*"A wise son heeds his father's instruction,
but a mocker does not listen to rebuke."*

You cannot get wisdom in isolation, for you need what
others have to be complete. Ultimately, your heavenly
Father oversees the process of your growth, and that
may include a timely rebuke from Him or others. **Are you**

resisting the process? Do you find reason to apply or dismiss what others say to you? Read Hebrews 12:4-13 to understand how and why God disciplines you.

June 14
Proverbs 14:23

"All hard work brings a profit,
but mere talk leads only to poverty."

Many talk about what they will do 'one day' and then wait. Others talk, set goals and work hard toward their desired end. **To which group do you belong?** Don't ever be satisfied with talk, for actions always speak louder than words. Paul addressed this principle in 1 Corinthians 4:20 and Jesus did in Matthew 7:21-24.

June 15
Proverbs 15:3

"The eyes of the Lord are everywhere,
keeping watch on the wicked and the good."

Adam and Eve tried to hide from God in the Garden, which was futile behavior. The Lord notices the good and the evil done by all. When you do good to others, He counts that as doing something good for Him. **Why not put on a show for God today by loving others and doing good?** You can read more about God's attentiveness in Matthew 25:31-46 and Revelation 4:7-8.

June 16
Proverbs 16:32

"Better a patient man than a warrior, a man
who controls his temper than one who takes a city."

Patience trumps power and skill in God's eyes. There is only one way to develop patience and that is to confront your impatience, confess it and learn to keep your peace in situations beyond your control. **When does your temper get the best of you? Is it time to repent and ask for God's help?** You may also want to read Ephesians 4:26-27, Colossians 3:12 and James 1:19-20.

June 17
Proverbs 17:9

"He who covers over an offense promotes love, but whoever repeats the matter separates close friends."

It can be difficult to keep an offense to yourself, yet today's verse indicates that when you do, it is for the sake of love. **Are you willing to act right while being wronged?** Think of Joseph and how he treated news of Mary's pregnancy as an example of this in Matthew 1:18-19 and further words of advice in 1 Peter 3:8-12.

June 18
Proverbs 18:19

"An offended brother is more unyielding than a fortified city, and disputes are like the barred gates of a citadel!"

This verse states a simple fact: Disputes between family and close friends can be intense and take a long time to reconcile. **Is there someone with whom you need to seek reconciliation?** It is not easy to achieve, so be patient. Remember Saul and Barnabas, whom God joined together but a dispute tore apart. If that happened to spiritual giants, it can easily happen in your world. You can read their story in Acts 13:1-3 and Acts 15:36-41.

June 19
Proverbs 19:21

*"Many are the plans in a man's heart,
but it is the* **Lord's** *purpose that prevails."*

It is common to preface plans with the word maybe.
"Maybe God wants me to do this or *maybe* go there."
God does not deal in 'maybes.' He is direct and specific.
**God is talking; are you listening? Are you acting
on what you hear?** The only way to cut through your
hesitancy is to face your fears and engage your purpose!
No more excuses! You can hear this truth in the words
Mordecai spoke to his cousin Esther in Esther 4:12-14.

June 20
Proverbs 20:6

*"Many a man claims to have unfailing love,
but a faithful man who can find?"*

Not everyone has the same talent, but talent may or
may not make you a valuable team member. If you
are faithful to encourage, punctual, ready to serve
and cheerful, and do those things day in and day out,
you will be a cherished member of any team, whether
at work or church. **Are you working on your talent
or your faithfulness?** Read how Peter declared his
commitment to Jesus in John 13:37-38 and then faltered
in faithfulness in John 18:15-27.

June 21
Proverbs 21:5

*"The plans of the diligent lead to profit
as surely as haste leads to poverty."*

Diligence is following through on commitments, promises and goals, regardless of how long it takes or what obstacles you encounter. Haste involves looking for shortcuts to success, of which there are none. And diligence usually leads to successful execution of the plans you make. **Are you a talker or doer? Diligent or impatient?** Read Hebrews 10:35-39 and determine if you are looking for shortcuts or ready to endure for the long haul.

June 22
Proverbs 22:26-27

"Do not be a man who strikes hands in pledge
or puts up security for debts.
If you lack the means to pay,
your very bed will be snatched from under you."

You cannot want something for others more than they do. Don't try to cover others' debts, whether natural or spiritual, even if they are family. If they are irresponsible, you can easily lose your money, your peace or both! Stop fretting, let their problem go, and focus on your own. **Are you minding your own business or straying into that of others?** Read Galatians 6:1-5 and see how it relates to today's passage.

June 23
Proverbs 23:4

"Do not wear yourself out to get rich;
have the wisdom to show restraint."

You need money, and God promises to provide it. Therefore you work to extend God's kingdom, not to amass riches or to meet your needs, for God can provide without your job. Perhaps it's time to ask: **Do you own your stuff or does your stuff own you? Do you work for money or does your money work for you?** This truth is reiterated throughout the Bible, including Deuteronomy 6:10-12 and Deuteronomy 8:16-18.

June 24
Proverbs 24:16

"For though a righteous man falls seven times,
he rises again,
but the wicked are brought down by calamity."

Failure and setbacks are part of every believer's life. They do not indicate you have done something wrong, but are opportunities for God to prove His faithfulness to you. If circumstances have you down right now, be encouraged, for you will rise again! Read how Paul encouraged the saints with this truth in Acts 14:21-22 and take it to heart today!

June 25
Proverbs 25:6-7

"Do not exalt yourself in the king's presence,
and do not claim a place among great men:
it is better for him to say to you, 'Come up here,'
than for him to humiliate you before a nobleman."

How do you feel when you are overlooked for a promotion, raise or project you would like to work on? Have you put your career and future in His hands, trusting Him for the progress? Read Psalm 75:6-7 and the story of Joseph and his promotion in Egypt in Genesis 37 through 50. If you don't have time for all that, then at least read Genesis 50:15-21.

June 26
Proverbs 26:12

"Do you see a man wise in his own eyes?
There is more hope for a fool than for him."

All of us are smarter than one of us. If you want excellence, you need to expand your team of workers, advisers and consultants so you can draw from a larger variety of life experience and viewpoints. **Do you consult with others as you plan your work or ministry, or does insecurity and pride make you a one-person team? How well do you collaborate with others as you carry out your work?** You can see the scope of Paul's network in Romans 16:1-16.

June 27
Proverbs 27:4

"Anger is cruel and fury overwhelming,
but who can stand before jealousy?"

It is all too easy to gossip, backbite or be sarcastic because you are jealous of someone's looks, gifts or popularity. Joseph's brothers were jealous of his coat and the Jewish leaders were jealous of Jesus' ministry success. **Is jealousy affecting your behavior in any way? Is another's jealousy impacting your own life or work?** You can read comments on and effects of jealousy in Acts 7:9-10, Acts 17:5 and Galatians 5:19-21.

June 28
Proverbs 28:14

"Blessed is the man who always fears the Lord,
but he who hardens his heart falls into trouble."

You can harden your heart or keep it pliable and tender toward the Lord. **If you are 'in trouble' right now, maybe it's time to stop looking 'out there' for the reason and instead look inside your own heart for the source of the problem?** You can find out what Jesus said about this matter in Mark 7:20-23.

June 29
Proverbs 29:25

"Fear of man will prove to be a snare,
but whoever trusts in the Lord is kept safe."

Fear of others' disapproval or criticism is a great hindrance to a productive life. **What could you do if you were not afraid of what others may say? How much time do you spend trying to figure out what someone may think or say if you do something? Is that really the way you want to live your life?** Jesus also had something to say about this in John 5:41-44.

June 30
Proverbs 30:5-6

"Every word of God is flawless, he is a shield to those who take refuge in him. Do not add to his words, or he will rebuke you and prove you a liar."

It's important you know God's Word and not be casual toward its interpretation. **What are you doing to increase your knowledge and understanding of God's Word? How much time do you invest in reading and studying the Bible? Are you doing extra reading or taking classes? As you learn, are you teaching others?** Read what Peter and Paul said about God's Word in 2 Peter 1:19-21 and 2 Timothy 3:16-17.

A Daily
Taste Of
Proverbs

July

July 1
Proverbs 1:1-2

"The proverbs of Solomon son of David, king of Israel: for attaining wisdom and discipline; for understanding words of insight."

These verses set forth the purpose for Proverbs, which is simple, easy to understand and focused. **Do you know your purpose? Do you know your organization's purpose? Can you describe them in one simple sentence?** If you are not clear on purpose, you are not clear on life! For additional insight on purpose, read Luke 7:30, Acts 13:36 and Romans 9:17.

July 2
Proverbs 2:10

"For wisdom will enter your heart, and knowledge will be pleasant to your soul."

Wisdom and knowledge are not 'head' things, but 'heart' things. They come not only from study but also from your experience as you follow Christ, learning from our success and failure. **Are you growing in wisdom and knowledge? How can you tell whether or not you are?** You may want to read more about this at Colossians 2:2-3, Ephesians 5:15-20 and James 1:5-8.

July 3
Proverbs 3:17

"Her [wisdom's] ways are pleasant ways, and all her paths are peace."

Is your life and work pleasant? Do you have peace?

If the answer is 'no,' then you may not be following in wisdom's ways. **Why not ask God to show you where you are off the wisdom path and then have faith and courage to learn and walk in new attitudes and behaviors?** To help understand today's verse, read Jesus' words in Matthew 11:28-30 and John 16:12-14.

July 4
Proverbs 4:22

"For they [words of wisdom] are life to those who find them and health to a man's whole body."

Spiritual illness can be a root cause of physical illness. **Do you think you are experiencing any current ailments because you have not confronted and dealt with sources of stress, anxiety, anger or fear in your life?** If so, then your cures are not to be found in earthly doctors but the Heavenly One. You may also want to read Romans 8:5-11 to learn more about the spiritual cure for your physical problems.

July 5
Proverbs 5:21

"For a man's ways are in full view of the Lord, and he examines all his paths."

You know what you do is always in full view of the Lord, but you may not always act like it. He knows what you did and why you did it. Don't act like you can escape accountability for your deeds. **With that in mind, what good deeds can you do today that will make your Heavenly Spectator enjoy what He sees?** Take a look at Matthew 6:3-5 and Hebrews 4:12-13, which also reminds you that God is watching!

July 6
Proverbs 6:16, 19

"There are six things the Lord hates,
seven that are detestable to him:
[one of those things is]
a man who stirs up dissension."

God loves those who promote harmony and unity. Anyone who gossips, spreads rumors or broadcasts damaging truths is not on God's list of favorites. Make sure you are not a source of division anywhere. Better yet, make sure to be a source of harmony and peace! 1 Corinthians 3:1-9 and 1 Corinthians 11:17-19 shows what Paul said about division and unity.

July 7
Proverbs 7:4

"Say to wisdom, 'You are my sister,'
and call understanding your kinsman."

The media is filled with stories of celebrities in business, music and athletics who lack wisdom, and some lose their lives because of it. Wisdom is to be like part of your family, and not just a casual acquaintance. **Are you making good decisions that honor God? Are you living a life that reflects godly wisdom in relationships, finances and work?** For some advice on how to live wisely read 1 Peter 4:7-11.

July 8
Proverbs 8:13

"To fear the Lord is to hate evil;
I [the Lord] hate pride and arrogance."

Are you always 'right'? Do you look down on or criticize others, especially leaders? If you don't deal with arrogance in your life, God will, because He hates it. It is your choice: Humble yourself or risk humiliation! The Bible has much to say about pride. Two significant statements are in Luke 1:50-52 and Luke 18:9-14.

July 9
Proverbs 9:1

"Wisdom has built her house;
she has hewn out its seven pillars."

When you live in the house wisdom has built for you, you are in a safe and secure place. Wisdom begins with the fear of the Lord and ends in right living. **Do you exhibit this wisdom in your relationships, work, finances and life decisions? Can you give an example of how you have done so in the last few days?** Jesus talked about a house of wisdom in Luke 6:47-49 and you would do well to heed His words.

July 10
Proverbs 10:25

"When the storm has swept by, the wicked are gone,
but the righteous stand firm forever."

The wicked and righteous both encounter life's storms. The difference is the righteous endure by God's grace but the wicked are undone. It may seem like your present storm will never end, but it will. God will make sure of it and preserve you in the process. You can read about the firestorm that will test your life and work in 1 Corinthians 3:10-15 and then look at how Job handled his storms in Job 1.

July 11
Proverbs 11:24

"One man gives freely, yet gains even more; another withholds unduly, but comes to poverty."

You never lose anything when you give. Even though you feel like you are losing something, you are really gaining. **How generous are you with your money, time, gifts and talents? Could some of your lack be due to stinginess? How can you cultivate a heart and culture of giving in your organization and family?** Jesus made a promise to those who are generous in Luke 6:37-38.

July 12
Proverbs 12:11

"He who works his land will have abundant food, but he who chases fantasies lacks judgment."

Your 'land' is your purpose, and if you find and 'work' it, you will have plenty of joy, peace and creativity. If you pursue fantasies not related to who He created you to be, you will be unhappy. **Do you know your purpose? Are you fulfilling it?** For example of someone working their 'land' of purpose, read Acts 9:36-41.

July 13
Proverbs 13:20

"He who walks with the wise grows wise, but a companion of fools suffers harm."

Everyone needs counsel and advice from time to time. **Have you established relationships with mentors** and coaches? Perhaps there is an author who speaks into your life? Is the company you keep able to help you get to the next level of purpose and productivity? If not, perhaps it's time to keep better company? You need the kind of advice from others that Jethro gave Moses as described in Exodus 18:12-27 if you are going to be wise and fruitful.

July 14
Proverbs 14:15

"A simple man believes anything,
but a prudent man gives thought to his steps."

The decisions you make today determine your effectiveness and success tomorrow. Some people do nothing and expect God to use and bless it! They believe that somehow they will write, build, go or grow with little or no effort. Others believe they will reap where they have not sown. **What are you doing today to make your tomorrow possible?** Paul announced that he was ready to receive his crown because he had run his race in 2 Timothy 4:6-8. **Are you running yours?**

July 15
Proverbs 15:23

"A man finds joy in giving an apt reply,
and how good is a timely word."

Encouragement is oxygen for the soul. Your mission today is to find those who need a timely word and give it to them! If you can't say it in person, then write or call them. You want to hear from someone soon, "Wow, I needed to hear that. Thanks!" To better understand the importance of encouragement, read Hebrews 3:12-14.

July 16
Proverbs 16:23

***"A wise man's heart guides his mouth,
and his lips promote instruction."***

Teaching is a 'heart' thing and not just a 'head' thing.
Also, don't underestimate what God has done in your life
and the power it can have to help and change others.
Look for opportunities to give away to others what God
has taught you through teaching, coaching or writing.
Read 1 Corinthians 14:26 and Colossians 3:15-17 to
understand God's expectations for you as a teacher.

July 17
Proverbs 17:3

***"The crucible for silver and the furnace for gold,
but the Lord tests hearts."***

God's 'tests' are not exams, but rather life situations that
reveal what is or is not in your heart. Often God tests
you to show you and those around you the work He has
done in your life. **Are you being tested right now?** If
so, God is just showing off His handiwork in you for all
to see, including principalities and powers who did not
honor God as you are doing. To better understand this
process, read James 1:12 and 1 Peter 4:13.

July 18
Proverbs 18:23

***"A poor man pleads for mercy,
but a rich man answers harshly."***

When you think you have it 'together,' you can look down

on, judge or speak harshly to someone who doesn't. **Have you forgotten the condition in which the Lord found you? Are you no longer mindful of your poverty before God, and your desperate need for God's grace?** If you need grace, then you should also be willing to give grace. You can read about your need to give mercy in Jesus' words in Matthew 18:21-35.

July 19
Proverbs 19:2

"It is not good to have zeal without knowledge, nor to be hasty and miss the way."

You can be sincere and be sincerely wrong! Don't think that sincerity will ever be an acceptable excuse for wrong action. Don't be in a hurry to proceed until you know what you should do, but once you know God's will, don't delay either. Read Malachi 2:7-8 to understand your need for knowledge and then look at how Paul waited and acted quickly in Acts 16:6-10.

July 20
Proverbs 20:24

"A man's steps are directed by the Lord. How then can anyone understand his own way."

You must trust the Lord and not fret about your career, relationships, money or ministry. Today you may not see the whole picture, but eventually you will. Be faithful where you are, and have faith that God knows how to get you where you need to be. You can see this happening in Samson's life in Judges 14:1-4, when he was being led and was not even conscious of what the Lord was doing. **Where may it be happening in yours?**

July 21
Proverbs 21:2

---

*"All a man's ways seem right to him,
but the Lord weighs the hearts."*

Some people are concerned about whether or not their actions are God's will, but never stop to ask if fear, pride, unbelief, racism or laziness are an issue when they make decisions. Don't ask God what you should do; rather ask Him to show you your heart. Often when you see that, you will know what to do - and what not to do! Reading Jeremiah 17:9-10 and Matthew 12:33-35 will give you a better understanding of this concept.

July 22
Proverbs 22:19

---

*"So that your trust may be in the Lord,
I teach you today, even you."*

It is wise to put your faith in God, not only as an event from time to time, but as a lifestyle. **Do you trust God today more than you did yesterday? What proof is there that you do? What are your faith goals that only God can help you achieve? What are you trusting the Lord for that you will look foolish if He doesn't come through?** Read what James had to say about faith and action in James 2:14-24 and then see how you can act out your faith today.

July 23
Proverbs 23:18

---

*"There is surely a future hope for you,
and your hope will not be cut off."*

No matter how bleak your world looks today, it can all change tomorrow with one meeting, phone call or idea. It may look impossible to you, but nothing is impossible for God. Don't abandon your hope, and next week or year at this time you may marvel at where you were and how far you have come! Read Jeremiah 32, Luke 1:47 and Jude 24-25 and stir up your hope in God today.

July 24
Proverbs 24:27

"Finish your outdoor work and get your fields ready, after that, build your house."

You must have priorities in life and work. If everything is important, then nothing is and, what's more, little gets accomplished. **Are you working toward short-term relief of pressing problems, or long-term projects that will bring lasting results? Do you go to bed feeling like you got nothing done, or are you confident at the end of the day that you were true to your values and priorities?** Jesus had priorities and spoke of how to set them in John 8:28-29 and Luke 12:35-38.

July 25
Proverbs 25:9

"If you argue your case with a neighbor, do not betray another man's confidence."

Sometimes people need a safe place to talk. **Can you be that safe place? Are people's secrets and failures safe with you? Or do you regularly share what you know about someone with others?** You may wish to read Proverbs 16:28 and 1 Peter 4:8.

July 26
Proverbs 26:17

"Like one who seizes a dog by the ears is a passer-by who meddles in a quarrel not his own."

The lesson here is simple: Mind your own business. **Why get angry over things that don't pertain to you? In fact, why are you so angry about certain things at all?** Don't take up an offense that isn't yours and don't be so quick to offer opinions about matters that really don't affect you. For an example of someone who lost his life because he took on a "battle" not his own, read 2 Samuel 2:8-23.

July 27
Proverbs 27:10

"Do not forsake your friend and the friend of your father."

Maintaining a friendship takes time and effort. **Are there friends with whom you have lost contact? Why not get in touch with them today and start being friends again, not just in word, but in deed?** Better yet, just call or write your friend(s) today to say hello. Proverbs has a lot to say about friendship, as you can see in Proverbs 17:17 and Proverbs 18:24.

July 28
Proverbs 28:7

"He who keeps the law is a discerning son, but a companion of gluttons disgraces his father."

The Law directs you to treat your neighbor as yourself.

A glutton puts the focus for life squarely on his or her personal needs. What's more, if you hang out with selfish people, there is a good chance you will become selfish as well. **Are you a selfish 'consumer' or selfless lover of others?** Don't answer before you read Matthew 5:16-48 and Matthew 19:16-22.

July 29
Proverbs 29:23

"A man's pride brings him low,
but a man of lowly spirit gains honor."

Pride gains God's immediate attention, but only so He can humble you. The proud say in their heart, "I can do this" or "I earned that, I don't need God." You are wise if you humble yourself before He has to do it for you. **Has pride crept into your thinking, speech or behavior?** Ask God to show you the reality of your heart before you answer. Read Psalm 138:6-7 and Proverbs 3:34 to get more insight into how the Lord relates to the proud.

July 30
Proverbs 30:11

"There are those who curse their fathers
and do not bless their mothers."

One of the Ten Commandments is to honor your father and mother. **If your parents are alive, do you spend time with them even if you don't live with them? If not, in what tangible ways do you honor their memory? In either case, do you bless them for giving you life?** Do something today that communicates your love and respect for your parents. You may also wish to read Exodus 20:12 and Ephesians 6:1-3.

July 31
Proverbs 31:23

"Her husband is respected in the city gate, where he takes his seat among the elders of the land."

God may use you to serve behind the scenes and make someone else look good. **Can you be part of a team where others get the notoriety and credit, whether family, work or ministry?** This requires humility and grace while also taking satisfaction that you at least have influence. Read Galatians 5:13-15 and Proverbs 27:18 to understand what you need to be a good team player.

A Daily
Taste Of
Proverbs

August

August 1
Proverbs 1:10

*"My son, if sinners entice you,
do not give in to them."*

Peer pressure is a problem for young and old alike. If you are young, there is pressure to fit in by trying new and sometimes dangerous things. The peer pressure for the old is not to make a mistake or to conform to group standards. **Where is peer pressure robbing you of your individuality, creativity or purpose? Where is it preventing you from doing what God wants you to do?** Read the unusual story of the prophet who gave in to peer pressure in 1 Kings 13:1-26 and see how peer pressure cost one servant of God his life!

August 2
Proverbs 2:7

"He holds victory in store for the upright."

God is for you and not against you. He is not hiding His will or purpose, and certainly is not withholding His presence, guidance or grace. **Are you living a 'victorious' lifestyle? If not, what do you need to change to do so? Where are you lacking the results in your purpose or ministry that can and should be yours?** Paul wrote about this truth in Romans 8:31-39.

August 3
Proverbs 3:25-26

*"Have no fear of sudden disaster or
of the ruin that overtakes the wicked,
for the Lord will be your confidence."*

You are commanded *not* to live in fear, but to keep your trust in the Lord. **Where does fear rule your life? What are you prepared to do to be set free? What will you do once you are free?** You may want to do some Bible study on fear but in the meantime read 2 Timothy 1:7 and John 14:26-27.

August 4
Proverbs 4:12

"When you run, you will not stumble."

This verse does not say *if* you run, but *when*. Some have decided God's people only work at one speed - slow and deliberate. Yet there is a time to wait and a time to run. **When is the last time you ran - stopped deliberating and started acting?** Have confidence that when you run, your steps are just as sure as when you walk. For further encouragement to move quickly to do God's will, read Jeremiah 12:5 and Genesis 22:1-5.

August 5
Proverbs 5:10

" . . . lest strangers feast on your wealth and your toil enrich another man's house."

Are you working so hard for someone else that you have no time or energy for the things that matter most to you? Do your best efforts go to build the wealth and kingdom of another? Perhaps it's time to make changes and reserve some of your best energies and creativity for *your* purpose and what God gave you to do. Read Ecclesiastes 3:22 and Matthew 6:25-34 to encourage you as you take steps to change your workday world habits.

August 6
Proverbs 6:16-17

"There are six things the Lord hates,
seven that are detestable to him:
[one of these things is} haughty eyes."

Haughty eyes affect how you see things and cause you to consider yourself as superior and correct. God dislikes anyone with a proud outlook, who is always right with no room for mercy or grace. Haughty eyes also cause you to be condescending. **Where has your outlook been colored by a haughty attitude?** You can get more insight into pride at Micah 6:8 and Proverbs 16:5.

August 7
Proverbs 7:16

"I have covered my bed
with colored linens from Egypt . . ."

Egypt has many colorful attractions, but for the people of God, they are distractions. The writer of Hebrews reported that Moses refused the passing pleasures of sin in Egypt to serve God. You are wise when you do the same. **Where have the attractions of Egypt - money, prestige, relationships, entertainment - gotten hold of your attention and affection?** Hebrews 11:25-26 and 1 Corinthians 6:8-11 will help answer the question.

August 8
Proverbs 8:27

"I [wisdom] was there when he
set the heavens in place, when he
marked out the horizons on the face of the deep."

If you want what you already have, then keep doing what you have always done. You need wisdom to do new things or old things in new ways. You get this wisdom by asking God who gives it freely but you must have faith that He will give it to get it. Read Ephesians 1:7-10 and Ephesians 1:17-21 for additional insight into this process of how God gives wisdom, and pray to receive it!

August 9
Proverbs 9:9

"Instruct a wise man and he will be wiser still; teach a righteous man and he will add to his learning."

God can never get out of you what you don't take time to put in and that requires effort on your part. **What are you doing to add to your skill, learning, wisdom or expertise? Do you have a reading plan? A mentor? Do you take private lessons or classes to enhance your area of expertise?** Read Paul's advice in 1 Timothy 4:14-17 and what Peter wrote in 2 Peter 1:5-8 and then apply their advice to your life and work.

August 10
Proverbs 10:5

"He who gathers crops in summer is a wise son, but he who sleeps during harvest is a disgraceful son."

There are two billion people who have yet to hear the gospel. You should be praying, giving and/or going to help fulfill the Great Commission. **What are you doing to help spread the gospel to the nations in this time of great harvest? Can you do more than you are now?** Read Matthew 9:36-38 and Matthew 28:18-20 to get more insight into the urgency of the harvest.

August 11
Proverbs 11:3

"The integrity of the upright guides them,
but the unfaithful are destroyed for their duplicity."

Your values help you make daily decisions consistent with what is most important to you. This is called integrity. If you only talk about what is important but don't do it, you are duplicitous, which is just another word for hypocritical. **Where in your life are you talking about something being of value to you, but doing very little about it?** Read John 13:16-17 and Luke 12:47-48 to reinforce today's lesson.

August 12
Proverbs 12:7

"A slothful man does not roast his prey,
but the precious possession of a man is diligence."

It is fine to start a project, but is a valuable trait to see it through to the end. **Why don't you finish more of what you start? Of what are you afraid? Where have you broken promises to yourself and others concerning what you would do?** For reasons why you may not finish what you started, see Mark 4:1-20. To see an example of one who did finish her commitments, see Luke 2:36-38.

August 13
Proverbs 13:15

". . . the way of the transgressor is hard."

Jesus said, *"My yoke is easy and my burden is light"*

(Matthew 11:30). If that's not the case in your life, then ask, **"Whose yoke am I carrying?" How can you find that 'easy' yoke? Why is your way and life so difficult and trying?** Read the short book of Obadiah to understand that as you have done, it will be done unto you by the Lord Himself!

August 14
Proverbs 14:4

"Where there are no oxen, the manger is empty, but from the strength of an ox comes an abundant harvest."

You may try to keep your manger empty so to speak, careful not to do anything that causes you inconvenience. Yet new habits and skills can help you grow and become more productive. **Where are you playing it safe, possibly missing a chance for a new harvest or increase?** To better understand what this verse is trying to teach, take a look at Luke 19:11-27.

August 15
Proverbs 15:8

"The Lord detests the sacrifice of the wicked, but the prayer of the upright pleases Him."

Some teach prayer as a duty. Others make it a new system of works, saying God doesn't act until you pray. This verse tells you God delights in your prayer, that it is an expression of your love relationship with your heavenly Father. **Why not bring God pleasure today and every day by both talking and listening to Him?** Read 1 Thessalonians 5:16-18 to gain insight into how Paul approached prayer.

August 16
Proverbs 16:7

---

*"When a man's ways are pleasing to the Lord,
he makes even his enemies to be at peace with him."*

If you make your focus pleasing the Lord, then God will
be involved in your daily affairs and relationships. The
word of God outlines the behaviors that please the Lord.
**Why not do a study of every verse that uses the
words 'pleasing' or 'please' the Lord and see what
you learn?** Take a look at 2 Corinthians 5:9 and then
see this verse in action in 2 Samuel 7:1-17.

August 17
Proverbs 17:16

---

*"Of what use is money in the hand of a fool,
since he has no desire to get wisdom."*

The rich young ruler kept the commandments, but was
attached to his money and could not follow Jesus. **Is
your money a source of anxiety for you, or a source
of blessing for you and others? Do you own your
money or does your money own you?** Read the
young man's story in Luke 18:18-25 and see if you
identify with his life and struggle.

August 18
Proverbs 18:2

---

*"A fool finds no pleasure in understanding,
but delights in airing his own opinions."*

Your opinions are not infallible, and it is not an
inalienable right that you be heard on all matters. If

you seek first to understand others and the Lord, then you will earn the right to be heard. Sometimes picking up your cross involves being quiet and listening. **How effective are you as a listener?** Read Mark 9:7 and John 2:1-5 if you want help understanding the listening process that leads to success.

August 19
Proverbs 19:11

"A man's wisdom gives him patience;
it is his glory to overlook an offense."

The Bible gives much instruction on how to handle a personal offense. One way is to overlook it. When you are able to do this, it is a glorious event, for you act as God often acts. **How patient are you when your rights are wronged? Can you let it go or does it occupy your mind and emotions for some time afterwards?** This truth is repeated in Colossians 3:12-14.

August 20
Proverbs 20:23

"The Lord detests differing weights,
and dishonest scales do not please him."

The Lord expects you to have integrity in your business dealings, not using 'dishonest' scales to weigh out service and quality. **Do you use company property as your own? Is your work exemplary? Do you keep your word? Do you treat the public as you would like to be treated?** The Lord is interested in your answers! **Are you?** You may wish to read 1 Timothy 6:1-2 and 2 Thessalonians 3:6-13 for more advice on the topic of work ethics.

August 21
Proverbs 21:30

"There is no wisdom, no insight,
no plan that can succeed against the Lord."

God reigns in the affairs of men. There is no world system or philosophy that can withstand His majesty. What's more, He rules in your life too, and you need not be afraid. If circumstances seem to indicate otherwise, read Psalm 91 over and over again. For good measure, read Revelation 19 and see how the Lamb is victorious over all opponents.

August 22
Proverbs 22:1

"A good name is more desirable than great riches;
to be esteemed is better than silver or gold."

What do you want your legacy to be when you are gone? If you amass wealth and prestige, you may be remembered for what you had. If you bless as many as possible while you are here, you will be remembered for who you are. I choose the latter. **Which do you choose?** You may want to read 2 Timothy 1:15-18 to see Paul's testimony about a man with a good name.

August 23
Proverbs 23:19

"Listen, my son, and be wise,
and keep your heart on the right path."

It requires effort to maintain a pure heart on a righteous path. Solomon prayed for wisdom, but he literally prayed for a 'listening heart.' **How well do you listen to God? How well do you listen to others?** How well do you **listen to your own heart?** Read Solomon's prayer in 1 Kings 3:7-10 and then see what Jesus told the crowd in Matthew 15:10.

August 24
Proverbs 24:6

"For waging war you need guidance, and for victory many advisers."

You need a personal board of directors who can advise you on various aspects of your life and work. These advisers can be alive and well, or role models who left a legacy from a life well lived. **Who serves on your personal board of directors? What difference are they making in your life?** As an example of one who sought advice and one who did not, read 1 Kings 22. **Which one would you prefer to have on your board of directors? Why?**

August 25
Proverbs 25:12

"Like an earring of gold or an ornament of fine gold is a wise man's rebuke to a listening ear."

Feedback from others, sometimes known as criticism, is a valuable thing, not to be taken lightly. If you do not want or seek feedback, however, you can see it as an unwelcome intruder. **How can you be more open to hear and receive what will only make you more effective, even if it can be difficult to hear?** Read what David said about feedback in Psalm 141:5 and then pray it yourself!

August 26
Proverbs 26:22

"The words of a gossip are like choice morsels;
they go down to a man's inmost parts."

It can be difficult to resist gossip, whether giving or receiving, just like it's hard to to pass up good food! **Why not choose today to harness the positive power of 'reverse' gossip and spread a good report about someone, building up his or her character and reputation in the eyes of others?** There was negative gossip about John the Baptist and Jesus as you can see in Luke 7:33-35. To see the power in positive 'gossip,' read Acts 9:26-30.

August 27
Proverbs 27:18

"He who tends a fig tree will eat its fruit,
and he who looks after his master will be honored."

It requires humility and grace to serve someone else's vision, working for them like you would for the Lord. Yet God promises honor for those who do. **Where or who is your fig tree? How is your attitude as you serve? Do you keep in mind that you are honoring God as you honor His servants?** Read about the woman who anointed Jesus in Matthew 26:6-13 and also what Isaiah said in Isaiah 26:13.

August 28
Proverbs 28:18

"He whose walk is blameless is kept safe,
but he whose ways are perverse will suddenly fall."

You may think you are not being observed, but you are. God is watching, and He will either preserve you, if your ways please Him, or trip you up, if your ways are not what they should be. You can't fool God. **Is there any area where you are actually sabotaging your own success?** To see someone who suddenly fell due to perverse ways, take a look at a man named Haman in Esther 7.

August 29
Proverbs 29:18 (KJV)

"Where there is no vision, the people perish."

Vision is important for an organization or an individual. **What do you see yourself doing in five years? Where are you living? What price are you willing to pay to get there? What things must you do to fulfill that vision?** Now ask yourself the same questions concerning your company, organization or ministry. Read Joseph's 'vision' in Genesis 37:1-11 and then meditate on how that vision impacted the rest of his life.

August 30
Proverbs 30:10

"Do not slander a servant to his master, or he will curse you, and you will pay for it."

If you have a problem with anyone, the best, but not always easiest, way to handle it is to go to them. Don't take your 'bad report' to others or even to God, that person's 'master.' **Is it time you stopped complaining to God about someone and set up an appointment to see him or her?** You can read how Jesus said to handle this problem in Matthew 5:22-24.

August 31
Proverbs 31:19

"Speak up and judge fairly;
defend the rights of the poor and needy."

A rich man's money can defend his interests, but the poor must rely on others to speak on their behalf. **What are you doing to help the poor and needy? Is there any way you can speak out on their behalf? How can you do that more often and effectively?** You may wish to read how Elijah employed his prophetic ministry on behalf of the poor widow in 1 Kings 17:7-24 and then prayerfully consider how you can use your own gifts to help the poor in your own way.

A Daily
Taste Of
Proverbs

September

September 1
Proverbs 1:8

"Listen, my son, to your father's instruction and do not forsake your mother's teaching."

Teaching is best done in a family setting, whether the natural family or the Church. **Are you being true to what your parents and spiritual parents taught you? Whether or not they taught you, are you now teaching others, especially your own children and grandchildren?** Read Proverbs 22:6 and Psalm 78:2-6 and then get about the work of teaching the next generation in some capacity.

September 2
Proverbs 2:21

"For the upright will live in the land, and the blameless will remain in it."

God makes a place for the righteous. For some it is a place to live and thrive. For others, it is a place of purpose and meaning. For all who trust Him, it is a place of security in His love and saving grace. **Are you living to the fullest in your land today?** Read how Joshua and Caleb inherited their land in Numbers 14:21-24 and notice it was faith that enabled them to live there.

September 3
Proverbs 3:5

"Trust in the Lord with all your heart and lean not on your own understanding."

A spiritual lie tells you that God cannot be trusted and

you must take matters into your own hands. When you do that, it leads to anxiety, worry and stress. This verse **commands** you to trust the Lord with all your heart. **Do you? Where is there evidence that you are trusting him? In your finances? Relationships? Career?** Read Hebrews 11:1-6 and be reminded that without trust and faith, it is impossible to please the Lord.

September 4
Proverbs 4:7

"Wisdom is supreme; therefore get wisdom. Though it cost all you have, get understanding."

There is a price to pay to get wisdom. Perhaps it is missing your favorite TV show, humbling yourself, or even going back to school. **What price are you willing to pay to get wisdom and understanding? Why do you desire them? What will you do with them once you get them?** Read Matthew 16:24-25 and see that any spiritual benefit is going to cost you something.

September 5
Proverbs 5:13-14

"I would not obey my teachers or listen to my instructors. I have come to the brink of utter ruin . . . ."

If you are to grow, you must continue to learn. And if you are to learn, then someone must teach you. **Do you have a teachable spirit? Can you receive from others easily and with grace? Who are your favorite teachers who always seem to have a 'word' for you?** If you don't learn and grow, you are actually resisting God, who is the One teaching you through others. To verify that truth, read Matthew 4:23 and John 6:45.

September 6
Proverbs 6:22

"When you sleep, they watch over you."

When you sleep, God does not. When you cannot do anything for yourself but rest, God can take action on your behalf. **Why do you allow anxiety and worry to rob you of sleep?** Take comfort from Psalm 127:1-2 and then study Philippians 4:8-9 to see if your thoughts, which you can control with God's help, are your source of anxiety or of peace.

September 7
Proverbs 7:8

"He was going down the street near her corner, walking along in the direction of her house . . . ."

The young man in this verse was heading to a place he should not go. **Are there 'places' you should not go, like television, the Internet, a neighbor's home or the mall?** If you have a weakness or an addiction, then you must be careful to avoid any path that leads to your problem. Read Matthew 5:29-30 and understand how ruthlessly you must deal with any source of temptation, whether it be a person or place.

September 8
Proverbs 8:15

"By me kings reign and rulers make laws that are just."

Wisdom equips you to be an effective leader. It enables you to make decisions today that are the right ones for tomorrow. Wisdom comes from learning and experience; sometimes even failure. **What are you doing to increase your capacity to lead others? Do you desire to be a leader? Why or why not?** See the wisdom David and Solomon had as young leaders in 1 Samuel 17:26-37 and 2 Chronicles 1, and follow their example of prayer and action in your own leadership style.

September 9
Proverbs 9:17

"Stolen water is sweet;
food eaten in secret is delicious!"

One of the problems with the 'passing pleasure of sin' is that it doesn't last. Secret sins may feel good at first and give some satisfaction, but they almost always have a way of going public. The best thing you can do is repent before the fruit of those sins forces you to in a more public arena. **Do you have any need of repentance from secret sins today?** In support of today's theme, read Isaiah 30:12-15 and follow its directives.

September 10
Proverbs 10:7

"The memory of the righteous will be a blessing."

It is never too early to think about the legacy you would like to leave behind. Author Stephen Covey recommended you write your funeral eulogy *today* and start earnestly doing what you want to be remembered for when you are gone. Read Nehemiah 13 and see how many times Nehemiah asked the Lord to remember him for the work he did. **What legacy do you pray God will enable you to leave behind and be remembered for?**

September 11
Proverbs 11:8

---

*"The righteous man is rescued from trouble,
and it comes on the wicked instead."*

This verse does not say that the righteous won't be in trouble; it says that God will rescue them when they are in trouble. What's more, encountering 'trouble' does not indicate you have done something wrong or that God is displeased. Finally, the wicked are the ones who will encounter the ultimate and inescapable trouble, not you. There is no better example of this than Daniel in the lions' den as told in Daniel 6.

September 12
Proverbs 12:6

"The words of the wicked lie in wait for blood . . . ."

There is an evil being in the world who doesn't just want to hurt you, he wants to destroy you, as Jesus warned. Don't underestimate the powers arrayed against you or their hatred of God, and don't ignore the fact that you need to trust in the Lord if you are going to survive their evil designs against you! **Where in your life are you encountering an attack of the enemy? What must you do to be delivered?** Read 1 Peter 5:8-9 and do what it says.

September 13
Proverbs 13:6

"Righteousness guards the man of integrity . . . ."

Integrity is regularly doing what is consistent with

unselfish and God-honoring personal values, especially when no one is watching or will know the decision you have made. **Have you thought and written out your values? Do you have a network of ethics that guides and guards you in the affairs of life, especially when you are tempted to take a moral shortcut?** For an example of one man with integrity and one without, read 1 Samuel 11.

September 14
Proverbs 14:32

"When calamity comes, the wicked are brought down, but even in death the righteous have a refuge."

You have hope no matter how bad your situation is because you have a place to go in times of trouble. What's more, death is not the end; it is only a transition if you know the Lord. **Are you living in hope? If not, why not? If so, with whom can you share your hope today?** Perhaps Jesus' words in Luke 12:4-7 will serve to boost your hope today. Then you can talk yourself out of depression or hopelessness as David did in Psalm 42.

September 15
Proverbs 15:5

"The cheerful heart has a continual feast."

Joy is both a decision and a gift. The Holy Spirit gives joy but you must choose to be joyful in the midst of all circumstances. Today's verse tells you this joy provides many benefits, like a feast for the soul. **Would others say that you are a joyful person?** Don't let grumbling or anxiety rob you of your joy today. To read more about joy, look at Galatians 5:22-23 and John 15:11.

September 16
Proverbs 16:4

"The Lord has made everything for its own purpose, even the wicked for the day of evil."

God is a God of purpose. He has assigned something for you to do only you can do, something for you to be only you can be. **Do you know your purpose? What price are you willing to pay to discover it? If you know it, are you fulfilling it to the max?** Look at some men of purpose as described in Exodus 9:15-17 and Galatians 2:6-8 to see what you can learn.

September 17
Proverbs 17:10

"A rebuke impresses a man of discernment more than a hundred lashes a fool."

An old saying states, "A word to the wise is sufficient." **How well do you take correction from others? How many people are close enough to you to deliver a meaningful rebuke? Do you have feedback systems set up in your life so you know how well you are doing?** Read how David handled his rebuke from Nathan the prophet in 2 Samuel 12:1-14 and see what you can learn and apply to your own life.

September 18
Proverbs 18:10

"The name of the Lord is a strong tower; the righteous run into it and are safe."

You are not to take the Lord's name in vain, which

doesn't refer to swearing or cursing. Rather you are to take and use it for His purpose and glory through prayer, right deeds and behavior. **What are you doing with and in the name of the Lord? Is it a refuge and tower, or only something you mention as you conclude your blessing over food?** Take some time to read what the apostles did with and in the name of the Lord in Acts 3:16 and Acts 4:7-12.

September 19
Proverbs 19:17

"He who is kind to the poor lends to the Lord, and he will reward him for what he has done."

When you give to those who cannot repay, it is like you are giving to God Himself! He keeps a record and repays you in due time with interest. **What more can you do for the poor not only today but on an ongoing basis?** To see an example of God watching and rewarding a generous person, read about the impact of one man's regular gifts to the poor in Acts 10:1-6.

September 20
Proverbs 20:4

"A sluggard does not plow in season; so at harvest time he looks but finds nothing."

If you want to reach a goal, you must employ dreaming, planning and diligence. If you break down in any of those three, you will not see the end result of your goal. **Which of those three do you need to engage today? Where is the breakdown in your attempt to set and achieve a goal?** Read Habakkuk 2:1-4 to understand the proper way to set and the steps required to achieve any goal.

September 21
Proverbs 21:22

---

*"A wise man attacks the city of the mighty
and pulls down strongholds in which they trust."*

You are involved in a spiritual war and must not take a passive role. **Is your prayer life making a difference in your community, family and world around you? Are you praying only for personal protection or are you pushing back forces of evil with which you come in contact?** An example of this in Acts 16:16-19. You can also read about aggressive prayer in Colossians 4:2-4.

September 22
Proverbs 22:13

---

*"The sluggard says, 'There is a lion outside!'
or 'I will be murdered in the streets!'"*

A lazy person's creativity is often channeled into excuse-making. Yet his or her laziness is often rooted in nothing more than fear. **What are you afraid of that is keeping you from taking steps to achieve your dreams and purpose? What creative excuses are you offering to justify your inactivity?** Read what Jesus said about excuses in Matthew 8:18-22 and then confront yours to overcome your sluggardly ways.

September 23
Proverbs 23:10

---

*"Do not move an ancient boundary stone
or encroach on the fields of the fatherless."*

This verse urges you to maintain integrity in the affairs

of life, for God is watching. Respect others' property as your own, whether you know them or not. Especially don't take advantage of the weak or the poor for your own personal or business gain. For an example of someone who did not heed this warning, read 1 Kings 21 and see how he was punished for his theft.

September 24
Proverbs 24:3

"By wisdom a house is built,
and through understanding it is established."

Proverbs explains that wisdom is to fear the Lord and understanding is how that fear applies to daily living. If you want to build something - a business, ministry, or family - you will do well to put God first and keep Him there, not just on Sunday but every day of the week. Take a look at what Jesus had to say about 'building' in Matthew 7:24-29 and then assess what kind of foundation you have laid for your life and work.

September 25
Proverbs 25:11

"A word aptly spoken is like apples of gold
in settings of silver."

What a word picture this verse paints! When you say the right thing in the right setting, it's like precious metals grandly displayed. **Are you a source of discouragement or encouragement for others?** Your uplifting words hold tremendous riches for others. Think of people you can write, call or visit today to give them an encouraging word! Take to heart what Paul said about your words (and other things) in Ephesians 5:3-5!

September 26
Proverbs 26:7

---

*"Like a lame man's legs that hang limp
is a proverb in the mouth of a fool."*

If you don't have the character or integrity to go with
your wise words, you lack moral authority. If you don't
know when or how to say something, you can say right
things, but they won't be effective. **How influential do
you want to be?** Let your life be your message and
your words will have added power and influence. Read
Leviticus 2:13 and Colossians 4:6 and meditate on what
it means to have your life and words 'salted.'

September 27
Proverbs 27:5

"Better is open rebuke than hidden love."

If love is really love, it cannot be hidden. It will act to
benefit the one who is loved. You cannot say you love
God but not His people. In other words, you cannot be a
loner Christian. You must be part of a church fellowship,
where honesty may be part of expressed love. **What are
you doing to show love for God's people?** John wrote
about loving God and His people in 1 John 2:9-11, which
you will do well to read and apply.

September 28
Proverbs 28:23

---

*"He who rebukes a man will in the end
gain more favor than he who has a flattering tongue."*

Yesterday you saw that hidden love is no love at all.

Today you see that lovingly confronting someone in the wrong can be a long-term strategy to win their favor and respect. **Is it fair to say that those who love will be those who rebuke and correct because they care?** Read Ezekiel 33:1-6, which describes the need to 'blow the trumpet' for those who are in spiritual danger, and then apply what you read to your life and work.

September 29
Proverbs 29:1

"A man who remains stiff-necked after many rebukes will suddenly be destroyed – without remedy."

There are limits to God's patience. If you continually ignore His warnings about your behavior or attitude, you run the risk of humiliation. Better to humble yourself than to be humiliated! **Is there an area of life you have resisted changing?** Read 1 Peter 5:5-7 and Matthew 21:44 and get busy loosening up that stick neck of yours!

September 30
Proverbs 30:2

"I am the most ignorant of men;
I do not have a man's understanding."

It is good to be realistic and know what you have, what you know and who you are by God's grace. If you don't, then you can be arrogant and rash, ignoring your limitations and weaknesses. **Do you understand God is the source of your life and success? Do you have a good idea of your strengths and weaknesses?** Read what Paul wrote about this topic in Romans 12:3-8 and then be about the business of being who you are, who God made you to be.

A Daily
Taste Of
Proverbs

October

October 1
Proverbs 1:28

"Then they will call on me but I will not answer;
they will look for me but will not find me."

This only happens when God repeatedly calls to you but you don't respond. Then one day you call on Him and He doesn't respond. **Are your prayers being answered? Does it seem like God is far away? Could that in part be due to the principle in this verse at work in your life?** Read what the Lord said to Solomon in 1 Chronicles 28:9 and see if and how it applies to your life.

October 2
Proverbs 2:3

"And if you call out for insight
and cry aloud for understanding . . . ."

If you want to find your purpose or the answer to a tough, complex life question, you must seek the Lord with enthusiasm, diligence and determination. **With what question(s) are you seeking the Lord? Are you journaling what you hear? How long are you willing to seek, and with what intensity, to get the answers you need?** To encourage you as you seek, read Psalm 9:10 and Psalm 34:10.

October 3
Proverbs 3:6

"In all your ways acknowledge him,
and he will make your paths straight."

Guidance should not be a problem for you if you truly

want to know God's will. God will make your path clear, but you must trust He is doing that as you ask and pray. Otherwise you passively wait for Him to 'speak' to you, when He has already put what He wants you to do in your heart. **Are you waiting for a 'confirmation' that will never come because you already sense what you are to do?** Read Isaiah 41:12-14 and take courage that God is leading you by the hand, whether you feel like that is happening or not.

October 4
Proverbs 4:1

"Listen, my sons, to a father's instruction; pay attention and gain understanding."

Listen and pay attention - those are two admonitions you would do well to heed. **How well do you listen? Do you hear and retain the names of others? Do you hear and follow instructions? Why is this important?** It is critical because how you listen to others is indicative of how you hear the Lord when He speaks to you! Read Isaiah 55:3 and then what Paul wrote in 1 Corinthians 15:46 to see that first comes the natural and then the spiritual. If that's true, then 'natural' listening done well precedes 'spiritual' listening.

October 5
Proverbs 5:1

"My son, pay attention to my wisdom, listen well to my words of insight."

Prayer should not be a one-way communication or exercise. Don't just make your petitions when you pray, but also pay attention with an expectation that you will hear something. God is always 'broadcasting.' **Are you attentive and listening? When you pray, do you talk or listen? And what do you do with what you hear? Do you at least write it down?** If you want a good example of this dynamic, read Acts 10:9-23.

October 6
Proverbs 6:9

"How long will you lie there, you sluggard? When will you get up from your sleep."

Achievement and success are never accidents. They are the result of dreaming, planning and diligence. Yet laziness is seldom the problem. Fear masked as laziness usually is the cause of your inactivity. If you deal with the fear, you will cure your laziness! **What are you afraid of that is keeping you from fulfilling your dreams and goals?** Read Numbers 13:21-33 and see how fear kept Israel from entering into the Land God promised them, and then determine if fear-induced laziness is keeping your from your own land of promise.

October 7
Proverbs 7:2

"Keep my commands and you will live; guard my teachings as the apple of your eye."

God's commands are not burdensome. They are a joy and should be kept as such. **Where is your heart less than joyful in the service of and obedience to God? Are you giving, working, serving and worshiping as He would want you to do?** You can reinforce the lesson in this verse by reading 1 John 5:3 and Jesus' own words in John 14:15-24.

October 8
Proverbs 8:6

---

*"Listen, for I have worthy things to say;
I open my lips to speak what is right."*

God is always 'broadcasting.' He is speaking to you through circumstances, His Word and other people. **Are you listening? Do you even expect to hear? When you hear, what do you do with what you have heard? Act or wait?** Don't put your faith in your ability to hear; rather put it in God's ability and willingness to speak. This truth is also spelled out for you in Hebrews 1:1-2.

October 9
Proverbs 9:5

---

*"Come, eat my food and drink
the wine I have mixed."*

God sets a table where you can eat and drink of His goodness to your heart's content. There is no limit or end to His grace and mercy. **Is there anything in your life right now that would keep you from enjoying this feast God has prepared just for you?** Read Psalm 34:7-9 and the Song of Solomon 2:3-5, which both speak about 'eating' God's goodness.

October 10
Proverbs 10:21

"The lips of the righteous nourish many . . . ."

Whether teaching, preaching, writing, broadcasting, praying or encouraging, your words should touch many people for their good. Yet you can be paralyzed with fear of what others may think or by being self-conscious as you scrutinize what you were about to say. When that happens, you miss opportunities to nourish others with your words. **Are you using the full power of your 'lips' to bless people all over the world, or at least all over your world?** Read Matthew 10:26-28 and determine what obstacles exist that keep you from speaking boldly.

October 11
Proverbs 11:11

"Through the blessing of the upright
a city is exalted,
but by the mouth of the wicked it is destroyed."

Words have the power to build up or tear down. You have the potential to bless an entire city with your words! **How are you using this tremendous power to make a positive impact on large groups of people where you live, work or worship? What is your plan from this point forward to do so?** Read 1 Kings 4:29-34 to see how Solomon fulfilled the potential described in today's verse in his lifetime.

October 12
Proverbs 12:24

"Diligent hands will rule,
but laziness ends in slave labor."

There is one sure way to succeed and that is not to give up, no matter how difficult the goal may be, or how long it takes to accomplish. **Can people depend on you to do the job or does someone have to be assigned to you to make sure you follow through? Do you start well but finish poorly? Do you break promises**

to yourself and others concerning what you will achieve? For a good example of one who started well and finished even better, read about Caleb and his inheritance in Joshua 14:6-15 and 15:13-16.

October 13
October 13:4

"The sluggard craves and gets nothing, but the desires of the diligent are fully satisfied."

Proverbs often extols the benefits of diligence, a trait that always seems to be rewarded when it comes to setting and achieving goals. Some people, however, see goal-setting as unspiritual. If you don't set goals, however, then **why do you need diligence? Do you set goals and then are you diligent to see them completed? What are your current goals? Are you making progress or stuck?** Read what Jesus had to say about diligence and goal-setting in Luke 14:28-33 and then apply it to your life and walk.

October 14
Proverbs 14:6

". . . knowledge comes easily to the discerning."

When you develop spiritual discernment, you have the ability to know and understand all kinds of things. Adam and Eve tried to take a shortcut to this knowledge by eating from the tree of the knowledge of good and evil. You will develop your discernment by learning from your life experience, listening to the voice of the Spirit and by studying and trusting God's word. You can see two examples of spiritual discernment in Acts 13:6-12 and 1 Kings 3:16-28.

October 15
Proverbs 15:29

---

*"The Lord is far from the wicked,
but he hears the prayer of the righteous."*

What a privilege it is that God hears your prayers.
**Are you making the most of the opportunity to
communicate with the God of the universe? If so,
what you are talking to Him about?** Ask God difficult
questions and seek Him for the answers as well as
the ability to do great things! Read what Jesus said in
Matthew 18:18-20, what Paul wrote in Ephesians 6:18
and then apply what you read today!

October 16
Proverbs 16:9

---

*"In his heart a man plans his course,
but the Lord determines his steps."*

There is nothing wrong with planning as long as you
allow the Lord to direct your steps as you carry out those
plans. God is often directing your heart even during
the planning process, whether or not you sense His
presence, so don't be afraid to write down your dream
and how you think you can achieve it! **Do you avoid the
planning process? Do you think it is unspiritual?**
Read Genesis 28:10-17 and meditate on how it relates
to today's verse.

October 17
Proverbs 17:8

---

*"A bribe is a charm to the one who gives it;
wherever he turns, he succeeds."*

People are always looking for shortcuts to long-term success, but there are none. Integrity, hard work and honesty are the highways that lead to lasting, meaningful results. **Are you willing to follow their path to success or are you looking for an easier way?** You can see an example of this temptation and Peter's response to it in Acts 8:18-24.

October 18
Proverbs 18:20

"From the fruit of his mouth a man's stomach is filled; with the harvest from his lips he is satisfied."

You should keep your words soft and sweet just in case you have to eat them! What's more, you should fill your mouth with talk of God and His word as often as possible. **If you had to live off the fruit of your mouth, would you thrive or have an upset stomach? If you had to live off speaking God's word, would you have enough to satisfy your hunger?** For an example of someone eating God's words and then feeding others, see Ezekiel 3:2-4 and Revelation 10:10-11.

October 19
Proverbs 19:8

"He who gets wisdom loves his own soul; he who cherishes understanding prospers."

If you neglect the accumulation of wisdom and knowledge, you work against your own best interests. This may indicate you don't like who you are, which is basically telling the Lord He made a mistake when He made you as you are. **How has this personal hang up kept you from growing in the Lord?** It may be time to take to heart Psalm 139:14-16 and Matthew 22:38-40, noticing how loving others depends on loving yourself.

October 20
Proverbs 20:9

"Who can say, 'I have kept my heart pure;
I am clean and without sin?'"

The answer is: "No one!" You must be careful when confronting the sins of another, for you have plenty of your own. This is why Jesus spoke of taking the plank out of your own eye before tending to the speck in your brother's (Matthew 7:3-5). **Have you become arrogant or upset toward someone with a sin problem when you should be humble because of your own?**

October 21
Proverbs 21:19

"Better to live in a desert
than with a quarrelsome and ill-tempered wife."

This verse isn't endorsing desert-living. It is simply making a statement that living with someone who is contentious, complaining and angry is no fun. **What kind of partner are you in marriage, family, work or ministry? Are you a pain to live with or do you die to self to bless those closest to you?** Read what John wrote in 2 John 4-6 and live up to his command to love.

October 22
Proverbs 22:3

"A prudent man sees danger and takes refuge,
but the simple keep going and suffer for it."

There is no room for being passive where your spiritual life is concerned. It is important to recognize and respond to potential dangers where your family, business, personal life and ministry are concerned. This requires courage and confidence. **What are the greatest threats you are facing right now and how are you dealing with them?** Read Mark 9:22-24 and consider how to apply what Jesus said about dealing aggressively to problems and temptations in your life, work and relationships.

October 23
Proverbs 23:20

"Do not join those who drink too much wine or gorge themselves on meat."

It is possible to be a Christian and be selfish. You can concentrate on taking care of yourself at the expense of others around you, actually becoming a spiritual glutton - always feeding yourself and your needs. **What are you doing to share your blessings or do you keep them all for and to yourself? What can you do today to 'feed' someone else, instead of expecting to be fed?** Read what Paul wrote in Philippians 3:17-19 and notice that he was writing about believers!

October 24
Proverbs 24:11

"Rescue those being led away to death; hold back those staggering toward slaughter."

You are dealing with life and death issues every day, whether you realize it or not. People who don't know the Lord are in danger of spending eternity out of God's presence and favor. You have the words of life that can rescue them from their dilemma. **Are you sharing words of life with whoever will listen?** Read Ezekiel 22:30-31 and Isaiah 59:15-16 to encourage you in this important work of sharing truth with those who need it.

October 25
Proverbs 25:13

"Like the coolness of snow at harvest time is a trustworthy messenger to those who send him; he refreshes the spirit of his masters."

You have been entrusted with the message of life to give to others. **Are you being a faithful messenger of the good news you have received and live in?** If so, then you are not only a blessing to those who hear, but also to the One who gave you the message to deliver! To see an example of trustworthy messengers at work, take a look at Acts 4:23-31.

October 26
Proverbs 26:15

"The sluggard buries his hand in the dish; he is too lazy to bring it back to his mouth."

What a silly picture of someone who puts food on his fork but doesn't bring it to his mouth! Yet if you start something and don't finish it, you can be just as foolish. **What you are putting off finishing and what is stopping you from doing it? Where is laziness controlling your life?** Read what Hebrews 6:10-12 has to say about laziness, and then devise a plan to get over this trait that is keeping you from realizing the full potential God has assigned you.

October 27
Proverbs 27:23

---

*"Be sure you know the condition of your flocks,
give careful attention to your herds."*

This verse urges you to pay close attention to the things and people around you. **Are you in touch and walking in reality where your 'world' is concerned? Are you assuming things are good but they are really otherwise? What about those closest to you? Do you notice when they are down, sad or angry?** To do so you must be interested and take the time to see things through the eyes of others. For two examples of this practice, look at Nehemiah 2:1-5 and Luke 5:17-20.

October 28
Proverbs 28:1

---

*"The wicked man flees though no one pursues,
but the righteous are as bold as a lion."*

A lion is not timid, passive or easily intimidated. A lion goes where it wants, eats what it wants and sleeps when it wants. **What can you learn and apply from the lion's example today? How bold are you when it comes to your purpose and goals? How aggressive are you in evangelism and prayer?** Read 2 Corinthians 3:11-13 and Hebrews 4:16 to better understand how to express this boldness in your spiritual life.

October 29
Proverbs 29:16

---

*"When the wicked thrive, so does sin,
but the righteous will see their downfall."*

This explains why you can turn the other cheek and bless those who treat you badly, as Jesus commanded. Either they will repent or God will bring justice for what they have done, so either way you 'win.' **Can you trust that God will eventually make all things right and judge the wicked, thus freeing you to do good today to those who treat you badly?** Read Revelation 7:9-17 and be reminded that God is in control and will judge all living creatures with justice and equity.

October 30
Proverbs 30:3

"I have not learned wisdom,
nor have I knowledge of the Holy One."

The more you learn about God, the more you realize how little you know. It is important to walk in humility and have a proper assessment of your own spiritual poverty and God's grace toward you. **Is this what Jesus talked about when He mentioned, among other things, being poor in spirit in Matthew 5:1-10? If so, do you have an accurate understanding of your spiritual poverty and need for God?**

October 31
Proverbs 31:8

"Speak up for those who cannot speak for themselves, for the rights of all who are destitute."

The poor and outcasts have no one to speak up and stand for them. Jesus was clear that addressing their needs must be part of your life and work. We know this because His disciples made this work an important part of their ongoing ministry after He ascended.

What are you doing to help those who cannot help themselves? Read what James wrote about this activity in James 1:27 and James 2:1-4.

A Daily
Taste Of
Proverbs

November

November 1
Proverbs 1:13

---

*"We will get all sorts of valuable things
and fill our houses with plunder."*

This is the method of those who take shortcuts to wealth
by coveting and confiscating what belongs to others.
**What is your attitude toward money and wealth and
how to accumulate it? Are you looking for shortcuts
or earning it with hard work and integrity? Do you
plan to hoard or distribute your riches?** Deuteronomy
8:10-20 speaks about wealth and how you obtain it.

November 2
Proverbs 2:9

---

*"Then you will understand what is right
and just and fair."*

Guidance is easily available for those who follow the
Lord. If God wants you to do His will - and He does -
then He must reveal to you what His will is. You can
hasten the process by committing to do whatever God
wants you to do *before* you know what it is. The rest
is up to Him. To better understand this process, read
Deuteronomy 29:29 and John 7:17. **Are you afraid
to make that unconditional commitment to His will
before He reveals it to you?** If so, then that may be the
reason you haven't found it yet!

November 3
Proverbs 3:14

---

*"For she [wisdom] is more profitable than silver
and yields better returns than gold."*

Some people make their living buying and selling precious metals. **What if you decided to spend your life accumulating wisdom?** You would be richer than any of the rich! **What can you do to start or continue building up reserves of wisdom? How or where can you 'spend' or invest wisdom?** Read Psalm 37:30-31 and Psalm 49 to see that getting wisdom is an important goal if you serve and live for the Lord.

November 4
Proverbs 4:20

"My son, pay attention to what I say,
listen closely to my words."

God is the great Communicator. He speaks in a still, small voice as you read His word, listen to others, or pay attention to circumstances. If your heart is to hear, His heart is to speak. **Do you believe this? Are you listening and paying attention? Can you summarize what He is communicating to you at this point in your life?** It may boost your faith to read 1 Kings 19:7-18 and see how the Lord graciously spoke to Elijah when he was tired and depressed. That is the same way God can speak to you, if you have faith and are listening.

November 5
Proverbs 5:9

"Lest you give your best strength to others,
and your years to one who is cruel."

Where and in whom are you investing your life? To what cause are you giving your time, strength and energy? Jesus instructed His followers to invest in what is eternal and not what will pass away. **Perhaps it's**

time to assess if you are doing that effectively? Read Jesus' words on this matter for yourself in Luke 9:23-26.

November 6
Proverbs 6:8

"Yet it stores its provisions in summer and gathers its food at harvest."

The work habits of the ant are famous, but **are yours?** It knows what season it is and what needs to be done in each. **Do you know how to plan your work and work your plan? What short-term and long-term goals are you pursuing? What is your vision for the next five years?** You can see this practice present in Joseph's life in Genesis 41:25-40 and it got him a promotion!

November 7
Proverbs 7:19

"My husband is not at home; he has gone on a long journey."

In the midst of life's busy-ness, it is important to maintain priorities. **Are you 'at home' for those who need you? Are you available emotionally for those who love you or distant and preoccupied?** Peter spoke about family relationships in 1 Peter 3:1-7. Also, read the blessing the elders bestowed on Ruth and Boaz in Ruth 4:11-12. **Is that kind of blessing working in your own family?**

November 8
Proverbs 8:18

"With me [wisdom] are riches and honor, enduring wealth and prosperity."

Honor is a byproduct of wisdom, yet you may shun honor, considering it inappropriate to a life of faith. Wisdom also promises prosperity for those who have it, and you can be uncomfortable with that as well. **Is it wrong to expect benefits from a life of faith and wisdom? Is it wrong to enjoy them if they come? Are wisdom's riches only spiritual and intangible?** Read Isaiah 58:12-14 and Psalm 112 to gain more insight into wisdom's blessings and fruit.

November 9
Proverbs 9:2

---

*"She [wisdom] has prepared her meat
and mixed her wine; she has also set her table."*

When you read Proverbs, you see that wisdom is doing everything possible to woo and befriend you. You must actually work *not* to have a relationship with wisdom! Of course, the New Testament tells you that wisdom is not a 'thing' but the Lord Jesus Himself. **Are you dining at the Lord's table of wisdom?** You can read more about this meal prepared by wisdom at Psalm 23:5-6 and 1 Corinthians 1:28-31.

November 10
Proverbs 10:22

---

*"The blessing of the Lord brings wealth,
and he adds no trouble to it."*

One of the problems with wealth is the expense and stress required to maintain it. Today's verse tells you that God's wealth doesn't come with the usual trouble. **Are you ambivalent about having wealth? Is that the reason why you don't have any? What good**

could you do if you had more than you have now? Is
it possible that it is God's will for you to have it?
Perhaps it's time to ponder 1 Timothy 6:6-10, which tells
you that *money* doesn't cause your problems, but rather
the *love* of money.

November 11
Proverbs 11:25

---

*"A generous man will prosper;
he who refreshes others will himself be refreshed."*

God is watching when you give and He rewards your
generosity. That is why you need to give more than
others need to receive what you give, for the giver gets
the greater reward. **Who can you bless and refresh
today? How can you develop long-term habits of
generosity?** Read Acts 10:30-31 and see how God
refreshed Cornelius in part due to his generosity. Then
read 3 John 5-8 in The Message translation to see how
God commends those who share with others!

November 12
Proverbs 12:14

---

*"From the fruit of his lips a man is filled
with good things as surely as
the work of his hands rewards him."*

You can create a meaningful life not just by what you do
but also by what you say to others. Yours is not simply
to avoid saying wrong things but to speak positive,
uplifting things to yourself and others. **How fruitful are
your 'lips'? How can you make your speech more
productive?** You may want to look at Paul's admonition
to Timothy in 1 Timothy 4:12 and Titus 2:7-9.

November 13
Proverbs 13:2

"From the fruit of his lips a man enjoys good things."

This is the same principle you saw in yesterday's verse. The wisdom writer repeated the importance of the tongue again and again to help you understand how powerful your words are, for good or evil. **You may not be saying anything bad, but are you saying anything beneficial? If you are not enjoying 'good things' in your life right now, is your mouth the culprit?** Read what Jesus had to say about words in Luke 6:44-46.

November 14
Proverbs 14:9

"Fools mock at making amends for sin,
but goodwill is found among the upright."

To be upright is not to be perfect. When you are upright, you admit you have sinned and try to make amends for your misdeeds. **Is there anything you need to do today to right a wrong you committed?** For an example of this, look at what Zacchaeus promised to do in Luke 19:1-10. Zacchaeus was not a sinless man, but after his encounter with Jesus, he was upright!

November 15
Proverbs 15:6

"Better a little with the fear of the Lord
than great wealth with turmoil."

Today's verse advocates a simple lifestyle as opposed to one with a lot of things and the stress that can go with them. Jesus asked what good it does to have a lot of stuff and then lose one's soul in the process. **What price are you paying to get and keep goods and money that you want or have? Do you own your stuff or does your stuff own you?** You can read Jesus' words on this issue in Mark 8:35-38.

November 16
Proverbs 16:8

"Better a little with righteousness than much gain with injustice."

This verse isn't saying it's bad to have a lot, but better to have God along with the things of life, whether much or little. If you aren't careful, your 'stuff' can own you instead of you owning it. **What spiritual price are you paying to get and keep your 'stuff'? Are you gaining it at the expense of others? What are you doing to share your substance of life?** Read about a man who had to answer similar questions in Mark 10:17-23.

November 17
Proverbs 17:1

"Better a dry crust with peace and quiet than a house full of feasting with strife."

At times, financial or professional success comes at the expense of family life and relationships. **What adjustments do you need to make to nurture and restore a lifestyle that is conducive to love and harmony at home? Where do you need God's help to bring healing in your family?** You may wish to read 1 Timothy 5:4-8 and Malachi 4 to understand how important it is to take care of your family with God's help.

November 18
Proverbs 18:11

---

*"The wealth of the rich is their fortified city;
they imagine it an unscalable wall."*

Money can make you feel invincible and immune to
problems. Yet wealth can deaden you to your real
spiritual condition. This can happen not only to an
individual, but also a nation, as you can see in America.
This can happen not only to an unbeliever, but also a
believer. **Are you counting on money to be your help
or protection?** Read what the Lord said to arrogant
Israel when they used their wealth to bully the poor in
Amos 4 and then make sure you are not doing the same.

November 19
Proverbs 19:16

---

*"He who obeys instructions guards his life,
but he who is contemptuous of his ways will die."*

When you think you know better than anyone else, it can
be difficult to receive instruction or advice. Even when
you 'mess up,' you still may stubbornly cling to your
independent ways. **How open to input from others are
you?** Read what happened to King Rehoboam when he
did not heed the advice of others and what it cost him in
1 Kings 12:1-17. Then determine not to make the same
mistake yourself.

November 20
Proverbs 20:18

---

*"Make plans by seeking advice;
if you wage war, obtain guidance."*

The wisdom writer not only urged you to heed advice, he also directed you to seek it! Getting advice should be a way of life, not just for emergencies. **Is pride or fear keeping you from an enthusiastic wisdom-seeking lifestyle?** You can see an example of Paul seeking advice even though the Lord had revealed something to him in Galatians 2:1-10.

November 21
Proverbs 21:13

"If a man shuts his ears to the cry of the poor, he too will cry out and not be answered."

The poor are crying out for help, but are you listening? It is easy to tune out their cries, for their voices seem to be everywhere. The answer is not deafness, but selectively choosing a cause or causes that are close to your heart and acting to help the poor within those worlds. **What regular help do you give to the poor and needy?** Read Zechariah 7:10-14 and Luke 11:38-42 and act on your need to help the needy.

November 22
Proverbs 22:9

"A generous man will himself be blessed, for he shares his food with the poor."

This is the time of year when people think more of helping others. **What can you do between now and Christmas to share what you have with someone who has little or nothing?** There is a blessing in it for you when you do! When the Lord first presented the Law to Israel, much of it had to do with how to care for the poor as you can read in Leviticus 25:25-54.

November 23
Proverbs 23:5

"Cast a glance at riches, and they are gone, for they will surely sprout wings and fly off to the sky like an eagle."

If money is your goal, you are pursuing a moving target that comes and goes! Jesus urged you to store up treasures in heaven, not on earth since you cannot take anything with you when it's your time to go. **Are you using your earthly treasure to make deposits into your heavenly account or is wealth your final and only objective?** You can read Jesus' words on this in Matthew 6:19-24.

November 24
Proverbs 24:31

"Thorns had come up everywhere, the ground was covered with weeds."

Life, like farming, is a constant cycle of sowing and reaping. When you stop tending and sowing, whether it is financial or spiritual things, the weeds overtake your fields. **What are you harvesting these days? Do you have a bumper crop of good things or a field full of weeds due to laziness, neglect or fear?** You can read Paul's words in 2 Corinthians 9:6-15 to be further instructed in this spiritual truth.

November 25
Proverbs 25:21

"If your enemy is hungry, give him food to eat; if he is thirsty, give him water to drink."

You are to treat your enemies like friends, for this is just what God does! He causes the sun to shine on the just and the unjust. **How well are you treating both those who are not your friends and those who also may be mistreating you?** Read Jesus' instruction on how to relate to your enemies in Matthew 5:43-48 and what Paul wrote about the same in Romans 13:8-10.

November 26
Proverbs 26:27

"If a man digs a pit, he will fall into it;
if a man rolls a stone, it will roll back on him."

You cannot escape the fact that you reap what you sow. What's more, God responds to you the way you respond to Him! For example, if you are merciful to others, He will be merciful to you. So in some ways, you control how God reacts to you, once again reaping what you sow! If you are not getting back from life what you want, then perhaps you are the problem. More proof of this truth is in Psalm 18:24-27 and Psalm 41:1-4.

November 27
Proverbs 27:26-27

"The lambs will provide you with clothing . . .
You will have plenty of goats' milk to feed you
and your family . . . ."

Are you worried about provision? You need not be! The Lord knows how to provide for you and your family and for all the families under his care. To see an example of how He once did this, read 2 Kings 4:1-7 and then be encouraged that God can do the same thing for you whenever you need it.

November 28
Proverbs 28:27

"He who gives to the poor will lack nothing, but he who closes his eyes to them receives many curses."

When you ignore the poor, you are in trouble with God. When you take care of them, God takes care of you. **Can some of your current financial problems be due to your own neglect of those who are close to God's heart?** Find the poor someplace in your world today, bless them and keep on blessing them. Read God's instructions to Israel in Deuteronomy 15:7-11 and see that God has communicated his concern for the poor in the Old Testament Law!

November 29
Proverbs 29:7

"The righteous care about justice for the poor, but the wicked have no such concern."

The Bible is full of commands to care for the poor, and Jesus emphasized this ministry as well. **As you approach Christmas, what can you do to help the poor? What more can you do year-round to promote justice for the downtrodden or to help alleviate their suffering?** Read what Jesus had to say about this in Luke 12:22-34, then decide how you are going to fulfill it!

November 30
Proverbs 30:8

"Keep falsehood and lies far from me; give me neither poverty nor riches, but give me only my daily bread."

When you think of it, your needs for today should be your only focus. **Why fret about tomorrow?** Thank God for what you have today and trust Him for tomorrow's provision. Then work today on your integrity, even if you are experiencing lack. You can read more about this disciplined focus in Philippians 4:10-13 and also Ephesians 4:14-16.

A Daily
Taste Of
Proverbs

December

December 1
Proverbs 1:33

---

*"But whoever listens to me will live in safety
and be at ease, without fear of harm."*

The antidote for worry and fear is wisdom, but only if you listen and heed her advice. **Do you realize that worry isn't just a bad habit, but rather sinful behavior?** What's more worry is a choice, just like seeking and applying God's wisdom is also a choice. So choose wisely today as to how you will live. Read what Paul said about anxiety and worry in Philippians 4:6-7 and then adjust your behavior and attitude accordingly.

December 2
Proverbs 2:8

---

*"For he guards the course of the just
and protects the way of his faithful ones."*

God is guarding your way and course, which means you should be heading somewhere. If the Lord is protecting you, that implies some danger and risk along the way. **Do you know where you are going? Are you aware of God's grace watching over you? What are the dangers you are facing?** A reminder of God's protective power on the path of life is found at Isaiah 43:1-5.

December 3
Proverbs 3:23

---

*"Then you will go on your way in safety,
and your foot will not stumble."*

Once again, the Lord promises safety and protection as

you move forward in purpose. **So why are you afraid?** Step out and take action! What can you do today that will bring you closer to a goal or dream of yours? Read Deuteronomy 20:2-4 and 31:6 and have courage to act!

December 4
Proverbs 4:6

"Do not forsake wisdom, and she will protect you; love her, and she will watch over you."

If you treat wisdom properly, she will take care of you. She will watch over you and you won't even realize it. There are times when God is shaping and directing your thoughts and you aren't aware of it. But only if you apply yourself to follow His wisdom. **What are you doing to grow in, apply and dispense wisdom?** Read Titus 2 to get an overview of God's expectations as you mature in the Lord and His wisdom for life.

December 5
Proverbs 5:6

"She gives no thought to the way of life."

Do you give thought to your way of life? Are you happy and doing what you love? If you don't have a plan of what life road to take, any will do. **Where would you like to be years from now?** Read what Isaiah said about 'the way' in Isaiah 8:11, 26:7, 30:21 and 48:17.

December 6
Proverbs 6:4

"Allow no sleep to your eyes, no slumber to your eyelids."

There were times when Jesus made prayer a higher priority than sleep. When you have goals and priorities, they energize you and they usually empower you to do more than you ever thought possible. **So what is important enough to you that are you willing to lose sleep over it?** You can see what Jesus did all night one time in Luke 6:12. Notice also what He did after His all-night prayer meeting.

December 7
Proverbs 7:26

"Many are the victims she has brought down; her slain are a mighty throng."

Once you are a believer, you are in a war, whether or not you choose to participate. You have an intelligent spiritual enemy who does not want to see you succeed. You will overcome him by "the blood of the lamb and the word of [your] testimony" as stated in Revelation 12:11. **Are you using your war weapons effectively? When is the last time you shared your testimony?**

December 8
Proverbs 8:30

"I [wisdom] was filled with delight day after day, rejoicing always in his presence."

Wisdom brings joy and, in a sense, is joy, for it helps you live a godly life. What's more, wisdom is not philosophy but is an important expression of who God is and how He practically relates to mankind. **Do you have wisdom? What are you doing to give it away? What more can you do?** You can read about what your wisdom should look like and be doing in James 3:13-18.

December 9
Proverbs 9:3

**". . . and she [wisdom] calls from
the highest point of the city."**

Wisdom is broadcasting to any who will listen in the
midst of life's busy-ness. Yet there are many other voices
vying for your attention. **Are you listening? What are
you doing with what you are hearing?** Throughout
Revelation, John heard a loud voice from heaven as
depicted in Revelation 1:10. **Are you hearing this same
loud voice of wisdom? If not, why not?**

December 10
Proverbs 10:30

---

*"The righteous will never be uprooted,
but the wicked will not remain in the land."*

You are a plant, planted and rooted in spiritual and not
physical ground. When you are in Christ, no one or no
thing can uproot you. **Are you putting down the kind
of roots in Him that will bear much fruit?** Read Psalm
1, which talks about you being a tree firmly planted by
the waters. Then reflect about the stability and security
you have in Him by reading John 10:28-30.

December 11
Proverbs 11:14

---

*"For lack of guidance a nation falls,
but many advisers make victory sure."*

It can be difficult to admit you don't have the answers,
that you need the help of others (maybe even a lot of

'others') to make it in life. It can be especially challenging when you mess up and want desperately to redeem yourself by yourself. **Just how open are you to the advice of others?** Read the story of a young man who lost almost his entire kingdom because he did not heed his advisers in 1 Kings 12.

December 12
Proverbs 12:2

"A good man obtains favor from the Lord, but the Lord condemns a crafty man."

God favors those who put their trust in Him, but opposes those who trust their own abilities. In the long run, God can do much more for you than you can for yourself, but you must trust Him. **Why not let go of your own efforts to promote your best interests and do things God's way?** Read 1 Chronicles 5:18-20 and 1 Samuel 17:47 to see how God helped those who understood how to let him fight for them in their battles.

December 13
Proverbs 13:9

"The light of the righteous shines brightly, but the lamp of the wicked is snuffed out."

It may not seem like God is paying attention, but He always is. He is watching and evaluating the ways of all people. He preserves those who please Him, but opposes those who are godless and wicked. Keep on doing good and God will cause your light to shine for all to see! You can read about God's treatment of the wicked in Jeremiah 16:17-18 and how He deals with the righteous in 32:17-19.

December 14
Proverbs 14:33

---

*"Wisdom reposes in the heart of the discerning
and even among fools she lets herself be known."*

Some people are waiting to be more educated or
spiritual before they attempt something. You may already
have more in you than you think. **What is stopping you
today from expressing the wisdom you have? What
or who are you afraid of? What are you waiting for?**
For encouragement, look at Peter and how he expressed
what was in his heart in Matthew 16:13-20.

December 15
Proverbs 15:24

---

*"The path of life leads upward for the wise
to keep him from going down to the grave."*

Wisdom is practical and keeps you safe, alive and
growing. **Is your path of life upward or flat? Are you
growing in your knowledge of God? Are you fulfilling
your purpose? What goals can you set for the New
Year that will take you 'up and on' in the Lord?** Read
God's promises for you if you overcome the difficulties of
life in Revelation 2:26-29 and Revelation 3:11-13.

December 16
Proverbs 16:20

---

*"Whoever gives heed to instruction prospers
and blessed is he who trusts in the Lord."*

You must maintain a teachable spirit and not become an

island unto yourself. If you cannot receive from others, then you may not even be able to receive from the Lord Himself! **Where and when have you stubbornly resisted input from others? What has it cost you? Has that really been a reflection of your lack of trust in Him?** As an example of a man who did not heed advice and instruction, read about Pontius Pilate in Matthew 27:17-24.

December 17
Proverbs 17:22

"A cheerful heart is good medicine,
but a crushed spirit dries up the bones."

Your joy, or lack of it, has health and mental implications for good or bad. **Are you doing what you love? How can you do it more often? How often do you laugh? Are you depressed or in a strong frame of mind?** Perhaps some of your health or emotional challenges are directly tied to your lack of joy. It may help to read the truth about joy found in Nehemiah 8:9-10 and then to determine if you have God's strength for daily living.

December 18
Proverbs 18:15

"The heart of the discerning acquires knowledge;
the ears of the wise seek it out."

You cannot be passive and serve the Lord's purpose. You must employ 'constructive waiting' and seek out what you need to do to succeed in the future. **What are you doing to acquire knowledge and become better at what you do and who you are? What books are you reading? What classes are you taking?** Read

Daniel 1 and see how Daniel prepared himself for successful work in Babylon, then go do the same.

December 19
Proverbs 19:14

"Houses and wealth are inherited from parents, but a prudent wife is from the Lord."

The holidays are a time to express gratitude to the Lord for many things, including family and relationships. It's also time to tell your family you love and appreciate them. The greatest gift you can give your family this time of year is your attention. **What special expressions of love can you give this holiday season?** Read Proverbs 31:28-29 and then find ways to express your love for your family in the days ahead.

December 20
Proverbs 20:11

"Even a child is known by his actions, by whether his conduct is pure and right."

There are no age limitations in the purpose of God. He can use the young and the old alike, as we see in the Christmas story with Mary and Elizabeth. **Are you using age as an excuse for not doing more for the Lord?** You may want to read about those two women, one young and one older, in Luke 1:5-45.

December 21
Proverbs 21:23

"He who guards his mouth and his tongue keeps himself from calamity."

The worst part of saying the wrong thing can be how badly you feel after you made others feel badly, not to mention the trouble your words can cause. The only way not to cause problems with your words is to use your mouth to bless and not for selfish or mean-spirited reasons. **Is it time to post a guard over your mouth?** As a man who knew how to use his words to bless and encourage, check out Simeon in the Christmas story in Luke 2:25-35 and then follow his example.

December 22
Proverbs 22:2

"Rich and poor have this in common: the Lord is the maker of them all."

The Christmas narrative reinforces the truth that all men need a Savior. Both the poor shepherds and rich Magi came to find and worship King Jesus. **Are you preoccupied with your riches, or lack of the same, and thus shortchanging your spiritual life?** What's more, your bond with others is not your economic status, but your mutual relationship with the Lord. Read Romans 3:22-24 along with Matthew 2 and Luke 2 to see today's verse in the context of the Christmas story.

December 23
Proverbs 23:22

"Listen to your father, who gave you life."

Think about the people who have brought life and help to you at critical times. It is good to know who those people are and to draw on their help when needed. These folks may be in your family, but they can also be an author, a mentor, a friend or someone in ministry. **Who speaks to**

A Daily Taste of Proverbs

you and it brings vitality to your life and work? Do you recognize that it is the Lord oftentimes speaking to you through them? In the Christmas story, Joseph received supernatural advice, which he followed, and it saved his family's life (see Matthew 1:18-25, 2:13 and 2:19-20). Advice you receive may have the same effect, so listen carefully.

December 24
Proverbs 24:20

". . . And the lamp of the wicked will be snuffed out."

The Christmas story is one of good triumphing over evil. Herod tried to kill the baby Jesus and almost succeeded. Yet Herod died and his kingdom came to nothing, while Jesus and His flock live and reign forever! Jesus leads His people to victory in this life and the next, overcoming sin and death on their behalf. **Are you living in the fullness of this eternal victory?** Read 2 Corinthians 2:14 and 1 Corinthians 15:53-55 and be reminded of the victory over all things that you have in Christ.

December 25
Proverbs 25:3

"As the heavens are high and the earth is deep, so the hearts of kings are unsearchable."

A King was born 2,000 years ago and His name is Jesus. The goodness and mercy in His heart are unsearchable and endless, but the Word of God reveals and explains them both. Celebrate the birth of Christ today and every day, and never lose your wonder for the King of glory and His unsearchable love! Read Ephesians 2:3-5 and be reminded of His love for you!

182

December 26
Proverbs 26:6

"Like cutting off one's feet or drinking violence is the sending of a message by the hand of a fool."

This verse employs an extreme simile, but it shows that God highly values faithfulness to deliver His message of life in Christ. You carry the most important message that Jesus was born to save men from their sins. **Are you proclaiming it every chance you get? What more can you do in the coming year to proclaim God's goodness?** Read Psalm 119:46 and 1 Peter 3:15 to see the kind of eager response the Lord expects you to give to all who ask.

December 27
Proverbs 27:1

"Do not boast about tomorrow, for you do not know what day may bring forth."

You should live every day like it is your last, while at the same time setting ambitious long-term goals. **What can you do to maximize this day? What can you plan today that can be done in ten years, one day at a time?** To understand the tension between the long- and short-term, read James 4:13-17, and then 1 Kings 6:37-38 and 1 Kings 7:1-3 to learn of Solomon's long-term building program. **What can you do for the Lord in the next 13 years if you start today?**

December 28
Proverbs 28:7

"He who keeps the law is a discerning son."

You cannot become competent in anything by accident. If you are to keep the law, you must first know the law. **What goal can you set for next year that will give you more knowledge and understanding of God's word? What are your reading and learning goals?** Now is the time to give that some thought! Look at Colossians 1:9-12 and determine how you can achieve the spiritual growth goals Paul mentioned there.

December 29
Proverbs 29:3

"A man who loves wisdom brings joy to his father."

What you do impacts others closest to you, for good or not. Your love for wisdom and your desire to apply it will be a blessing to your family, whether natural or church. **How can you express your love for wisdom in the coming year in a way that will bring others help and joy?** Read James 3:17-18 to better understand wisdom and its traits and then set a course to obtain practical wisdom that will be a blessing to others.

December 30
Proverbs 30:4

"Who has established all the ends of the earth? What is his name, and the name of his son? Tell me if you know!"

If you were given a quiz on your faith and the Bible, how well would you do? What goals can you set in the coming year that will enable you to grow in the knowledge of your faith, the Bible and the Lord Himself? Your goals should not only be to increase learning, but to apply that learning to godly living. It is the longest psalm, but perhaps you can end the year by reading Psalm 119 and note the connection between the Word and holiness.

December 31
Proverbs 31:3

"Do not spend your strength on women, your vigor on those who ruin kings."

Your relationships should be godly and life-giving. **Are there any people in your life who are hindering your ability to go forward and be the person God wants you to be?** Then perhaps the coming year is when you make adjustments so you can give your energy and attention to your purpose and goals and not to so many dysfunctional people. You may want to see what Jesus had to say about your relationships in Matthew 10:34-39 and then make some changes based on what He said.

CONCLUSION

I hope you have enjoyed this version of my latest daily devotional. I was surprised at the level of excitement and engagement I enjoyed while compiling this work, even though I have worked with Proverbs as much as I have over the years. That is one of the beauties of God's word - it never grows old and we grow in our ability to learn and gain insight as we mature, study and apply the principles we find in all of God's word.

I want to express my love and appreciationg to my son, John III, who has edited this manuscript and prepared it for publishing. It did not escape my notice that Proverbs is a book composed by a family:

Listen, my sons, to a father's instruction;
    pay attention and gain understanding.
I give you sound learning,
    so do not forsake my teaching.
For I too was a son to my father,
    still tender, and cherished by my mother.
Then he taught me, and he said to me,
    "Take hold of my words with all your heart;
    keep my commands, and you will live"
(Proverbs 4:1-4).

To have my son working on something perhaps his children will work on as well is a rare privilege. Thank you, John, for your many hours devoted to editing and formatting this work. I hope it was an enjoyable experience for you.

And I hope this was also an enjoyable and learning experience for you and that you will share this book with others who may benefit. There are not many modern and relevant studies on the market today, and I am committed with my remaining days to produce as many as I can.

Thank you for reading and I pray you are equipped with more timeless wisdom to face your world and God.

A Daily
Taste Of
Proverbs

Scripture
References

Proverbs (cont.)

13:20	July 13
14:6	October 14
14:9	November 14
14:11	January 14
14:14	May 14
	August 14
14:15	July 14
14:22	March 14
14:23	June 14
14:26	February 14
14:29	April 14
14:32	September 14
14:33	December 14
15:1	January 15
15:3	June 15
15:5	September 15
15:6	May 15
	November 15
15:8	August 15
15:9	February 15
15:14	April 15
15:21	March 15
15:23	July 15
15:24	December 15
15:26	February 6
15:29	October 15
16:4	September 16
16:5	August 6
16:7	August 16
16:8	November 16
16:9	January 16
	October 16
16:20	December 16
16:21	April 16
16:23	July 16
16:25	February 16
16:26	March 16
16:28	July 25
16:32	May 16
	June 16
17:1	November 17
17:3	July 17
17:4	February 17
17:8	October 17
17:9	June 17
17:10	September 17
17:16	August 17
17:17	July 27
17:18	April 17
17:20	January 17
17:22	December 17
17:24	March 17
17:27	May 17
18:1	May 18
18:2	August 18

Proverbs (cont.)

18:5	February 18
18:9	March 18
18:10	September 18
18:11	November 18
18:12	April 18
18:13	January 18
18:15	December 18
18:19	June 18
18:20	October 18
18:23	July 18
18:24	July 27
19:2	July 19
19:3	April 22
19:3	May 19
19:8	October 19
19:9	February 19
19:11	August 19
19:13	January 19
19:14	December 19
19:15	March 19
19:16	November 19
19:17	September 19
19:21	June 19
19:25	April 19
20:4	September 20
20:5	March 20
20:6	June 20
20:9	October 20
20:11	December 20
20:12	April 20
20:18	November 20
20:21	May 20
20:23	August 20
20:24	July 20
20:25	January 20
20:28	February 20
21:1	May 21
21:2	July 21
21:4	February 21
21:5	June 21
21:13	November 21
21:16	March 21
21:19	October 21
21:20	April 21
21:22	September 21
21:23	December 21
21:30	August 21
21:31	January 21
22:1	August 22
22:2	December 22
22:3	October 22
22:4	February 22
22:6	March 22
	September 1
22:9	November 22

Proverbs (cont.)

22:12	April 22
22:13	September 22
22:19	July 22
22:20-21	January 22
22:26-27	June 22
22:29	May 22
23:1	April 23
23:4	June 23
23:5	November 23
23:10	September 23
23:10-11	January 23
23:12	February 23
23:18	July 23
23:19	August 23
23:20	October 23
23:21	March 23
23:22	December 23
23:23	May 23
24:1-2	March 24
24:3	September 24
24:6	August 24
24:9	February 24
24:10	May 24
24:11	October 24
24:14	January 24
24:16	June 24
24:20	December 24
24:27	July 24
24:31	November 24
24:32	April 24
25:1	January 25
25:2	May 25
25:3	December 25
25:5	February 25
25:6-7	June 25
25:7-8	April 25
25:9	July 25
25:11	September 25
25:12	August 25
25:13	October 25
25:21	November 25
25:27	March 25
26:4-5	May 26
26:6	December 26
26:7	September 26
26:12	June 26
26:14	March 26
26:15	October 26
26:16	April 26
26:17	July 26
26:22	August 26
26:24	January 26
26:24-25	February 26
26:27	November 26
27:1	December 27

Proverbs (cont.)	
27:2	May 27
27:4	June 27
27:5	September 27
27:7	January 27
27:8	February 27
27:10	July 27
27:12	March 27
27:17	April 27
27:18	August 27
	July 31
27:23	October 27
27:26-27	November 27
28:1	October 28
28:7	July 28
28:7	December 28
28:9	January 28
28:12	March 28
28:13	February 28
28:14	June 28
28:18	August 28
28:20	April 28
28:23	September 28
28:26	May 28
28:27	November 28
29:1	September 29
29:2	March 29
29:3	December 29
29:4	February 29
29:7	November 29
29:11	April 29
29:13	January 29
29:16	October 29
29:18	August 29
29:20	May 29
29:23	July 29
29:25	June 29
30:2	September 30
30:3	October 30
30:4	December 30
30:5	May 30
30:5-6	June 30
30:8	November 30
30:10	August 30
30:11	July 30
30:15	April 30
30:20	January 30
30:32	March 30
31:1	May 31
31:3	December 31
31:4	March 31
31:5	January 31
31:8	October 31
31:19	August 31
31:23	July 31
31:28-29	December 19

Ecclesiastes	
2	May 1
3:22	August 5
5:18	June 6
11:1-6	May 14

Song of Solomon	
2:3-5	October 9

Isaiah	
8:11	December 5
10:1-3	January 31
26:7	December 5
26:13	August 27
30:12-15	September 10
30:21	December 5
41:12-14	October 3
43:1-5	December 2
48:17	December 5
50:4-5	April 16
55:3	October 4
58:12-14	November 8
59:15-16	October 24

Jeremiah	
3:1-5	February 5
9:23-24	June 12
12:5	August 4
16:17-18	December 13
17:9-10	July 21
29:10-14	March 30
31:31-34	May 3
32	July 23
32:17-19	December 13

Ezekiel	
3:2-4	October 18
11:18-20	June 7
22:30-31	October 24
33:1-6	September 28

Daniel	
1	December 18
1:3-8	January 7
4	February 21
6	September 11

Joel	
2:12-13	May 4

Amos	
4	November 18

Jonah	
3	January 11

Micah	
6:8	August 6

Habakkuk	
2:1-4	September 20
2:2-4	January 22

Zephaniah	
3:17	May 8

Haggai	
1	April 10

Zechariah	
7:10-14	November 21

Malachi	
4	November 17

Matthew	
1:5	January 10
1:18-19	February 10
	June 17
1:18-25	December 23
2	December 22
2:5-12	April 24
2:13	December 23
2:19-20	December 23
4:23	September 5
5:1-10	October 30
5:16-48	July 28
5:22-24	August 30
5:29-30	September 7
5:43-48	November 25
6:3-5	July 5
6:19-24	November 23
6:20-22	January 24
6:25-34	August 5
7:3-5	October 20
7:21-23	January 28
7:21-24	June 14
7:24-29	September 24
8:18-22	September 22
9:36-38	August 10
10:26-28	October 10
10:34-39	December 31
10:37	April 17
10:40-42	June 11
11:28-30	July 3
11:30	August 13
12:33-35	July 21
13:1-23	April 5
13:44-46	June 2
15:10	August 23
16:13-20	December 14
16:24-25	September 4

Galatians (cont.)

2:11-14	April 19
5:19-21	June 27
5:13-15	July 31
5:22-23	September 15
6:1-5	June 22

Ephesians

1:7-10	August 8
1:17-21	August 8
2:3-5	December 25
2:8-10	April 26
3:7	March 26
4:11-24	April 8
4:14-16	November 30
4:17	April 2
4:26-27	June 16
4:28	May 10
4:29-32	January 15
5:3-5	September 25
5:5-7	February 26
5:15-17	March 9
5:15-20	July 2
5:21-33	February 12
6:1-3	July 30
6:4	March 22
6:18	October 15

Philippians

2:19-23	March 31
3:17-19	October 23
4:6-7	December 1
4:8-9	September 6
4:10-13	November 30

Colossians

1:3-6	May 5
1:9-12	December 28
2:2-3	July 2
3:9-10	April 13
3:12	June 16
3:12-14	August 19
3:15-17	July 16
3:18-21	January 19
3:21	March 22
3:22-24	May 10
4:2-4	September 21
4:6	September 26

1 Thessalonians

2:9	June 6
2:13	February 2
4:11-12	May 10
5:12-14	March 19
5:14	May 16
5:16-18	August 15

2 Thessalonians

1:4-11	May 24
3:6-13	August 20

1 Timothy

4:12	November 12
4:14-17	August 9
5:4-8	November 17
6:1-2	August 20
6:6-10	November 10

2 Timothy

1:7	August 3
1:15-18	August 22
2:2-7	March 23
2:14-26	January 8
3:16-17	June 30
4:6-8	July 14

Titus

1:1	May 6
1:6-9	March 29
2	December 4

Philemon

April 27

Hebrews

1:1-2	October 8
3:12-14	July 15
4:1-11	April 4
4:12-13	July 5
4:16	October 28
5:11-14	January 13
6:10-12	October 26
10:35-39	June 21
11:1-6	September 3
11:25-26	August 7
12:1-2	April 20
12:4-13	June 13
13:2	May 15

James

1:2-8	April 9
1:5-8	July 2
1:12	July 17
1:19-20	June 16
1:22-24	March 7
1:27	January 23
	October 31
2:1-4	October 31
2:1-13	January 29
2:14-24	July 22
3:3-6	April 12
3:5-10	June 10
3:13-18	December 8

James (cont.)

3:17-18	December 29
4:4-5	June 5
4:13-17	December 27

1 Peter

1:3-4	May 5
3:1-7	November 7
3:8-12	June 17
3:13-15	March 3
3:15	December 26
4:7-11	July 7
4:8	July 25
4:9	May 15
4:11	May 17
4:13	July 17
5:5-7	September 29
5:8-9	September 12

2 Peter

1:5-8	August 9
1:19-21	June 30
2:19	May 6

1 John

1:5-9	June 4
1:8-10	January 30
	February 28
2:9-11	September 27
2:16	April 18
3:1	May 8
3:11-18	April 3
5:3	October 7

2 John

4-6	October 21

3 John

5-8	November 11

Jude

24-25	July 23

Revelation

1:10	June 8
	December 9
2:26-29	December 15
3:11-13	December 15
3:17-19	May 23
4:1	March 5
4:7-8	June 15
5:12	June 8
7:9-17	October 29
10:10-11	October 18
12:11	December 7
19	August 21

ABOUT THE AUTHOR

John Stanko is the founder and president of PurposeQuest International, which creates resources and tools to help people around the world clarify their purpose and order their lives. He is a sought-after conference speaker and consultant, and his website and blog are popular sites where people go to better understand who they are and how to be more productive.

John resides in Pittsburgh, PA and earned his Doctor of Ministry from Reformed Presbyterian Theological Seminary. You can stay in touch with John's world through the following sites and radio shows:

www.purposequest.com

www.johnstanko.us

www.stankobiblestudy.com

www.stankomondaymemo.com

www.blogtalkradio.com/acacthreads

www.blogtalkradio.com/genevacollegemsol

or via email at johnstanko@gmail.com

John also does extensive relief and community development work in Kenya. You can see some of his projects at www.purposequest.com/contributions.

PurposeQuest International
PO Box 8882
Pittsburgh, PA 15221-0882

OTHER BOOKS BY JOHN STANKO

Life is a Gold Mine

I Wrote This Book on PurposeQuest

A Daily Dose of Proverbs

A String of Pearls

Strictly Business

Unlocking the Power of Your PurposeQuest

Beyond Purpose

The Faith Files: Volume One

The Faith Files: Volume Two

The Faith Files: Volume Three

Changing the Way We Do Church

The Revelation Project

The Price of Leadership

What Would Jesus Ask You Today?

Urban Heroes: Volume One

Urban Heroes: Volume Two

.